GLUTEN-FREE VEGAN BAKING
FOR EVERY OCCASION

GLUTEN-FREE
VEGAN BAKING
for Every Occasion

75 Classics & New Creations to Celebrate

Sara McGlothlin

Photography by Evi Abeler

ROCKRIDGE
PRESS

To my mom, for instilling in me a love for baking at an early age. And to Alex, for being my biggest cheerleader and most encouraging recipe tester.

Interior and Cover Designer: Michael Cook
Photo Art Director / Art Managers: Sara Feinstein and Sue Smith
Editor: Vanessa Ta
Production Editor: Erum Khan

Photography © 2019 Evi Abeler. Food styling by Albane Sharrard.

Author photo courtesy of Ash Carr.

Cover: Almond Bundt Cake with Vanilla Icing

ISBN: Print 978-1-64152-410-0 | eBook 978-1-64152-411-7

Contents

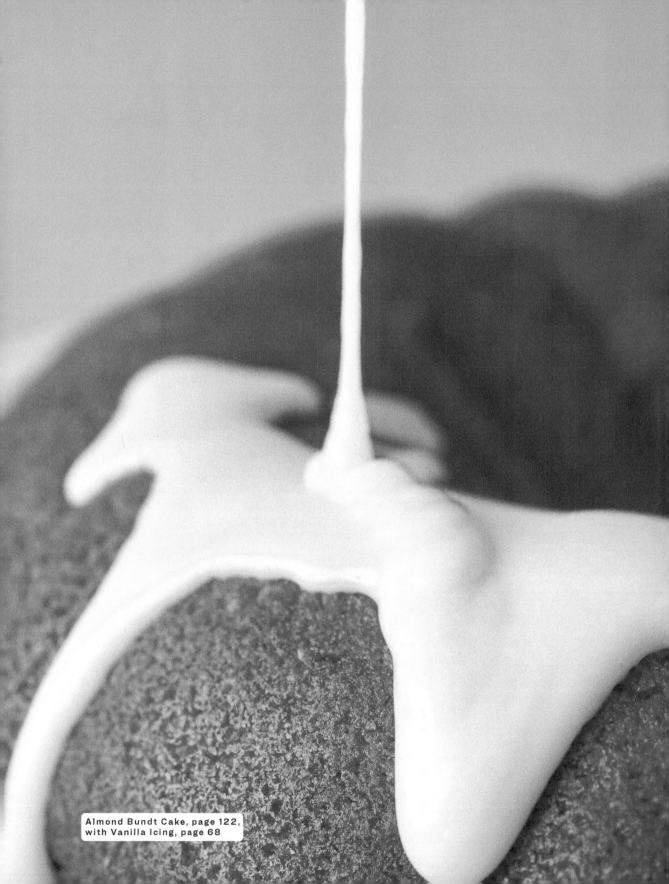

Almond Bundt Cake, page 122,
with Vanilla Icing, page 68

Introduction

My earliest memories of baking stem back to when I was about four or five years old. Wearing an oversized apron, I would assist my mom with holiday desserts, birthday cakes, and chocolate chip cookies to have on hand "just for fun." I always kept a notebook nearby, in which I would (pretend to) write down the recipe as we went. Cracking the eggs and helping my mom hold the hand mixer as we beat the batter were always my primary responsibilities. I now know that these experiences were so special not only because of the delicious result that came out of the oven but also because of the memories created right alongside the sweet treats.

As I got older, I continued to bake—although the recipes that I gravitated toward changed over time. In my early to mid-20s, I immersed myself in nutrition and health, and I became curious about the foods that worked best for my body. I eventually realized that the ingredients that I was accustomed to cooking and baking (gluten and dairy, specifically) were the root cause of my fatigue, digestive problems, and skin issues. I became certified as a holistic health coach, and I learned much more about the power of eating whole, real foods. I would spend the weekends experimenting in my kitchen, creating recipes comprised of those ingredients that better served me. I have realized that a few changes in my diet don't need to stop me from doing (and eating) what I love. Baking remains one of my favorite pastimes, an activity that gets me in the flow. For me, it is a hands-on sensory experience where time passes effortlessly.

I understand that many people share my story. Due to certain food allergies or intolerances, you may have felt forced into making a difficult dietary shift. As with any change, there can be an element of uncertainty. With dietary changes in particular (given that food and the way we eat can be deeply ingrained in childhood and tradition), perhaps there is a fear of missing out on those foods you know and enjoy. That is why I am so excited to share these recipes with you! They are proof that you can now bake delicious food similar to the traditional treats you have enjoyed in the past while staying aligned with your dietary needs and preferences.

Whatever your motivation for wanting to further explore a gluten-free and vegan way of eating, the fact that you are here is something to be celebrated! I hope that rather than feeling deprived, you approach these recipes from a mind-set of abundance. Also know that even if you have not strictly adhered to a gluten-free or vegan diet, I am confident you will still enjoy these baked goods. Either way, my ultimate hope is that you make these recipes in the same way they were created: with presence, pleasure, celebration, and love.

CHAPTER ONE

GLUTEN-FREE VEGAN BAKING

Through the gluten-free and vegan recipes found in these pages, I want to help you tell some new stories—those of comfort, celebration, and experience. As you re-create the baked goods I am sharing with you in your own kitchen, what takes shape is not just a tasty, sweet treat in one form or another but food that will forever be a part of a memory, whether that is a cake you make for a family member's birthday, the cookies you prepare for your child's annual bake sale, or the pie you bring to a backyard barbecue. It is my promise to you that the ingredients will not sacrifice flavor; better yet, they yield creations that support your health as well. Therefore, you can rest assured that these delicious and nutritious baked goods will serve you both physically and emotionally.

CELEBRATING OPTIONS!

These days, it is nearly impossible to separate food from feeling. Food is just as much a part of a celebratory time as the friends and family who gather around the table. Baking specifically is a modality meant for the more emotional side of life. We not only bake to eat, we also bake to preserve tradition, stir nostalgia, and cultivate joy.

I believe that our society is undergoing a shift in awareness around the food we eat and how it affects us. Not only is a plant-based way of eating becoming more common, but more people are also starting to realize that what you put in your body matters and that food is information for your cells. The hang-up when it comes to baking, however, is that many of the traditional ingredients used (conventional flours, refined sugar, dairy milk, and eggs) either are not tolerated by some people or are not included in a vegan diet. If either of these dietary restrictions applies to you, know that this does not mean you must forgo your favorite baked goods.

We are lucky to live in a time where we are becoming increasingly aware of alternatives, but our options can still feel limited when it comes to finding these foods on the market. This means that we must take matters into our own hands. With simple substitutions, we can upgrade ingredients so that you (or a loved one) do not have to miss out on this delicious slice of life. Gluten-free vegan baking can be fun and enjoyable, and this book is designed to show you how!

THE BASICS OF GLUTEN-FREE VEGAN BAKING

Often when one shifts to a particular diet, it can feel overwhelming and even isolating at times. Food is such a major aspect of the social side of life. Given that baked goods are something to be shared, I want to reassure you that these recipes were created with that in mind. Even those loved ones in your life who do not necessarily follow a gluten-free vegan way of eating will enjoy them too! Whatever the occasion that calls for you to bake, I hope the food that you create from these recipes will help you feel connected.

WHAT YOU NEED TO KNOW

If gluten-free vegan baking is totally new to you, I understand the concern about using ingredients you might not be accustomed to. Therefore, I outline everything you need to know, from the basics of gluten-free vegan baking, to how it compares to more conventional methods, to the equipment you will need to have on hand. I want to help make this transition as smooth as possible. I also want you to know that you do not have to completely overhaul your kitchen—just swap out some simple ingredients to reestablish your pantry. This will be a fun exploration of a more beneficial way of baking!

One of the major differences of going gluten-free compared to using traditional flours is in the texture. Gluten is a very sticky protein that provides strength and elasticity. Without gluten, baked goods can lack the binding aspect you might normally find when working with conventional baked goods, especially breads. As you mix the wet ingredients into the dry, the texture might not have that "pull" to it that you may be used to. I would describe it as feeling a bit more "fluffy."

This is where patience comes in to play! With many of these recipes, you must allow the batter to rest before baking. Letting it sit before transferring it to its cooking vessel gives the batter time to absorb the moisture and get a little sticky. Then, mixing with your spatula, you help alter the components of the delicate ingredients before the batter even goes in the oven. Don't worry—you will not have to wait too long; 20 to 30 minutes is sufficient, and the recipes will denote as much.

When baking gluten-free *and* vegan, you must make up for the absence of eggs and butter. A major question that comes up is how to replicate the taste and texture of yolks and the creamy, coating effect of butter, using purely plant-based ingredients. The use of flax eggs, full-fat coconut milk, and fruit and vegetable purées are all examples of how to achieve results that are just as delicious. I outline these techniques in the section on pantry items (page 7).

Along these lines, there are also many recipes that require refrigerating the dough before baking. Given the lack of traditional binders (e.g., eggs, cream, and butter), refrigerating the dough allows the fatty ingredients that are found in these recipes (coconut milk, coconut oil, and nut and seed butters, for example) to solidify and hold everything together. One important thing to note is that many of these baked goods might not rise in the way you are used to. You will notice that many of the recipes call for mixing the coconut milk or almond milk with an acid (such as vinegar or citrus juice) as one of the initial steps. This creates a "buttermilk" effect, which works with the leavening agent (baking soda and/or baking powder) to encourage rising.

ABOUT THE RECIPES

I am so excited for you to really dive in to these recipes! They are broken into their respective categories: Breakfast Bakes; Breads; Cookies, Brownies, and Bars; Cakes and Cupcakes; and Pies and Tarts. There will be gluten-free vegan versions of classic favorites as well as some new baking creations to add to your repertoire. Each recipe includes dietary labels
at the top (such as Grain-Free or Nut-Free), so you can know right away if the ingredients align with your needs. If applicable, substitutions are offered to give you options. You will also find tips and storage guidelines to help make your baking experience more enjoyable.

To make this cookbook as easy to use as possible, I have matched many of the muffins, cakes, cupcakes, cookies, and bars with my favorite topping, filling, and/or accompaniments within each recipe so you don't have to flip through the book looking for additional instructions. For this reason, you may notice that many of the staples, like glazes, frostings, and whipped creams, are repeated. While I have paired up my favorites, feel free to mix and match the frostings, icings, and glazes as you wish to create your own masterpieces. Or leave them off if you prefer!

One of my biggest pieces of advice is to read the *entire* recipe first. This small step can help you adequately plan and prepare, especially when the recipe calls for extra resting or refrigerator time. After reading the recipe, I also suggest you set out and measure all of your ingredients before you get started. This allows for a shorter and smoother preparation time. To help further set you up for success, I have listed some other suggestions in the pages that follow.

WHAT YOU'LL NEED

While you will not have to get overly fancy with your kitchen equipment, here are some items you want to have on hand, ranging from the basic baking essentials and very useful tools to items that are nice to have. I also provide a list of the pantry items frequently found in these recipes, along with their purpose. Having these items on hand will ensure you are prepared before you get started.

KITCHEN EQUIPMENT ESSENTIALS

- **Baking dishes.** An 8-by-8-inch baking dish is needed for many of the bar, brownie, and bread recipes. A 9-by-13-inch baking dish is used in several recipes as well.

- **Baking sheets.** I recommend having two large baking sheets.

- **Box grater.** Some recipes call for finely grating fruits and vegetables, like apples, zucchini, and carrots.

- **Cake pans.** I recommend having two 8-inch round springform cake pans. The majority of the cake recipes are double-layer cakes, so having two pans allows you to bake both layers at the same time. The springform feature allows for easy removal and serving. You can also use regular 8-inch cake pans, but I suggest lining the bottom with parchment paper before baking.

- **Can opener.**

- **Chef's knife.**

- **Cookie cutters.** A 2-inch cookie cutter is great to have when it comes to making Chocolate Cookies with Buttercream Filling (page 86). For making Sugar Cookies with Vanilla Icing (page 68), feel free to use any size or shape depending on the season or holiday!

- **Cutting board.**

- **Donut pan.** A standard-size donut pan is needed for Apple Cinnamon Donuts with Maple Glaze (page 26). Nonstick options come with either 6, 8, 9, or 12 cavities, so any of those will do.

- **Loaf pan.** The majority of the bread recipes use a standard loaf pan. I suggest using an 8½-by-4½-inch or 9-by-5-inch loaf pan.

- **Measuring cups and spoons.**

- **Mixing bowls.** I love the Pyrex three-piece mixing bowl set, and I suggest having one or two additional large mixing bowls as well.

- **Mixing tools.** While a hand mixer will work just fine, I absolutely love my KitchenAid stand mixer. It allows me to control the speed while freeing up both hands. Using the whisk attachment on an immersion blender works really well for making frostings.

- **Muffin tin.**

- **Parchment paper or aluminum foil.** For lining baking sheets and loaf pans.

- **Pie plate.** I suggest a 9-inch glass pie plate.

- **Rolling pin.**

- **Tart pans.** I use a 9-inch nonstick tart pan with a removable bottom. All tarts can be made in a 9-inch pie plate, but the crust recipe might yield a thinner crust in a pie plate. I also suggest having a set of 4-inch mini tart pans for Vegan Custard Mini Tarts (page 150). These mini tart pans normally come in a pack of six.

- **Wooden spoons and a wire whisk.**

NICE TO HAVE

- **Food processor.** I like the Cuisinart 14-cup food processor. Some recipes call for chopping dried fruit (as in Date Caramel Blondie Bars, page 82), and some batters can be more easily blended using a food processor (such as those that use thick nut butters or pumpkin purée). It's also an easy way to make your own gluten-free oat flour.

- **Food thermometer.** Helps determine if a baked good is done. The traditional toothpick test works, but when it comes to certain recipes, knowing the internal temperature of a bread or cake, for example, can provide you with a much more precise picture.

- **High-speed blender.** I have a Vitamix, and while it might be one of my more expensive pieces of equipment, it has been one of the best cooking investments I have ever made.

PANTRY ITEMS

- **Almond flour.** Made from ground almonds. The finely ground variety works well in baking. Know that there is a difference between finely ground almond flour and almond meal, which has a coarser texture and may lead to a heavier, grainier result. I recommend Bob's Red Mill superfine almond flour, which is made from blanched whole almonds. In general, almond flour is a more delicate flour to work with, so this is where letting the batter rest becomes crucial. Otherwise, you might find that your baked good will start to sink in the center as it cools.

- **Arrowroot starch.** Produced from finely grinding the root of the arrowroot plant. Like tapioca flour, it can be used as a thickener in gluten-free baking and as a replacement for cornstarch should you be watching your grain intake. Use 2 tablespoons arrowroot starch for every 1 tablespoon cornstarch, or you can substitute cornstarch one-for-one with tapioca flour.

- **Cocoa powder.** I recommend using natural unsweetened cocoa powder. Dutch-process (also called "alkalized") cocoa powder is darker in color and has been washed in an alkaline solution to neutralize its acidity, which may negatively affect your baked good's rising ability. You can also substitute cocoa powder one-for-one with raw organic cacao powder, which is chocolate in its most pure form.

- **Coconut flour.** Made from dried coconut meat. It has a sweet, nutty taste, and I love it as a grain-free flour alternative, especially for those who might be intolerant to tree nuts. Some recipes do call for it but only in small amounts, as it is very delicate and absorbent and therefore has a tendency to soak up too much moisture, which prevents baked goods from rising. Make sure the amount you use is precise, as laid out in a recipe—too much or too little can alter the outcome. Also, it is not to be substituted for other nut-based products but is intended to be used as a complement to other flours.

- **Coconut milk.** I love using full-fat coconut milk from the can (not the carton). It provides that fatty, creamy consistency that dairy milk normally provides. You can substitute it with almond milk or another dairy-free milk of choice, but these tend to have a thinner consistency, and the results will not be the same. Native Forest is my favorite brand of coconut milk.

- **Coconut oil.** These recipes primarily use melted coconut oil when this oil is called for. Given that it is more solid at room temperature, it must be kept in a warm place or heated to get it to its liquid form. I suggest using unrefined or virgin coconut oil, as *refined* means that the coconut has been baked and bleached and is therefore more processed. You can substitute it one-for-one for any other vegetable oil (e.g., olive oil or safflower oil). I also like to use nonstick coconut oil spray for greasing pans as well.

- **Fruit and vegetable purées.** Applesauce, pear purée, and pumpkin, sweet potato, and butternut squash purées are wonderful ways to add moisture and volume to your gluten-free and vegan baked goods. Mashed banana and avocado are amazing options as well. These ingredients also act as binding agents. You will find them used often throughout these recipes, and feel free to substitute any of them one-for-one with whichever you have on hand (but know that taste might differ slightly depending on what you use).

- **Gluten-free flours.** There are now options for all-purpose gluten-free baking mixes on the market. I find that many use bean flours as a base, and they can be a bit overpowering. I like to balance them out with brown rice flour or gluten-free oat flour (see how to make your own on page 49), but feel free to use only the mix if that is what you have on hand. Bob's Red Mill is my favorite brand.

- **Ground flaxseed.** These recipes frequently use flax eggs as a binding agent when baking. A flax egg is simply 1 tablespoon ground flaxseed mixed with 2 tablespoons water (some ratios are 1:2½ or 1:3, but I prefer 1:2 for a more gelatinous result). When mixed with water, ground flaxseed is a hydrocolloid, meaning it gels and therefore becomes an effective emulsifier. If a recipe calls for flax egg(s), you will find it listed early in the directions as it has to set for at least 10 minutes.

- **Sea salt.** While basic table salt will work fine in these recipes, I suggest using finely ground pink Himalayan sea salt. It is less processed, contains many minerals, and could make your food taste better.

- **Sweeteners.** Coconut nectar and maple syrup (not pancake syrup—I primarily use Grade A Amber Color maple syrup, but any Grade A or Grade B variety would work) are the main liquid sweeteners used in these recipes. You are welcome to substitute them one-for-one with another liquid sweetener of choice. Coconut sugar and monk fruit sweetener are the granulated sugars I suggest, but white sugar, cane sugar, or turbinado sugar work just as well. Just know that whatever you choose might alter the taste, texture, and color of your baked good.

- **Tapioca flour.** Also called tapioca starch, it is produced from the ground pulp of the cassava root. It is primarily used as a thickener in gluten-free baking and is a wonderful grain-free replacement for cornstarch (use 2 tablespoons tapioca flour for every 1 tablespoon cornstarch). I use it often, as it helps to bind and provide that chewy texture.

- **Vegan butter.** There are many options for vegan butter on the market that use nuts, like cashews, and/or coconut oil as a base. I like Miyoko's Kitchen brand, and Earth Balance and Melt are good too. There are even recipes out there to make your own using coconut oil and nutritional yeast. When a recipe calls for melted vegan butter, you can substitute with melted coconut oil, but it might result in a different taste and texture.

Have fun! Baking is supposed to be fun. Put on some music or a favorite podcast. Call on a friend or family member and make an activity out of it. Be present and enjoy the sensory experience of creating something delicious.

Apple Cinnamon Donuts with Maple Glaze, page 26

CHAPTER TWO

BREAKFAST BAKES

Peanut Butter Banana Bread

OIL-FREE • PREP AHEAD • SOY-FREE | **Makes:** 1 loaf (10 slices)

Prep time: 10 minutes, plus 30 minutes to rest
Cook time: 55 minutes | **Cooling time:** 2 hours 15 minutes
Equipment: Hand mixer or stand mixer, 8½-by-4½-inch or
9-by-5-inch loaf pan, food thermometer (optional)

There is nothing more comforting than a slice of banana bread in the morning. Adding peanut butter to the batter gives this traditional baked good a delicious flavor and a dense, moist texture. Enjoy with an extra pat of peanut butter and a sprinkle of cinnamon for a warming meal or snack.

½ cup full-fat coconut milk or unsweetened almond milk

1 teaspoon apple cider vinegar

1 cup brown rice flour

¾ cup almond flour or another gluten-free flour

3 tablespoons tapioca flour

⅓ cup coconut sugar or granulated sugar

2 teaspoons ground cinnamon

1½ teaspoons baking powder

½ teaspoon baking soda

¼ teaspoon sea salt

1 cup mashed very ripe banana (about 3 small or 2 large bananas)

⅓ cup creamy peanut butter or almond butter

1 tablespoon maple syrup

1 teaspoon vanilla extract

1. In a medium bowl, combine the coconut milk and vinegar. Whisk and set aside.

2. In a large bowl or stand mixer, combine the brown rice flour, almond flour, tapioca flour, coconut sugar, cinnamon, baking powder, baking soda, and salt. Stir until blended.

3. To the bowl with the coconut milk and vinegar, add the mashed banana, peanut butter, maple syrup, and vanilla. Whisk until creamy.

4. Pour the wet ingredients into the flour mixture, and beat until a batter forms. Allow the batter to rest in the bowl at room temperature for 30 minutes.

5. Meanwhile, preheat the oven to 350°F. Line a 8½-by-4½-inch or 9-by-5-inch loaf pan with parchment paper or spray with cooking spray.

6. Use a spatula to mix the batter a few times before transferring it to the prepared loaf pan. Bake for 40 minutes. Cover the pan with aluminum foil, and bake another 15 minutes, or until the internal temperature is between 190°F and 200°F or a toothpick inserted in the center comes out clean. Allow the bread to cool in the pan for 10 to 15 minutes before transferring to a wire rack to cool completely, about 2 hours.

Storage: Wrap the bread in plastic wrap or aluminum foil, and store at room temperature for up to 3 days.

Ingredient tip: While still in the peel, massage the banana with your hands until very soft. Scrape the contents into a bowl or measuring cup and mash with a fork until creamy.

Blueberry Muffins

GRAIN-FREE • OIL-FREE • SOY-FREE | **Makes:** 8 muffins

Prep time: 10 minutes | **Cook time:** 25 minutes | **Cooling time:** 1 hour 30 minutes
Equipment: Muffin tin, hand mixer or stand mixer

Blueberries are probably my favorite fruit. Not only do I love anything that reminds me of summer, but blueberries also pack a lot of nutrition in a tiny package, which makes me happy when I'm wearing my health-coaching hat. I recommend using fresh blueberries, if available, for this recipe. This will lead to a fluffier texture, and you will get a nice berry burst with every bite.

¾ cup full-fat coconut milk or unsweetened almond milk

1 teaspoon apple cider vinegar

1 cup almond flour

½ cup tapioca flour

¼ cup coconut flour

⅓ cup coconut sugar or monk fruit sweetener

2 teaspoons baking powder

½ teaspoon baking soda

¼ teaspoon sea salt

2 tablespoons coconut nectar or maple syrup

1 teaspoon vanilla extract

1 cup fresh or frozen blueberries (if frozen, thaw, rinse, and drain before using)

1. Preheat the oven to 350°F. Line a muffin tin with muffin liners.

2. In a medium bowl, combine the coconut milk and vinegar. Whisk and set aside.

3. In a large bowl or stand mixer, combine the almond flour, tapioca flour, coconut flour, coconut sugar, baking powder, baking soda, and salt. Stir to blend.

4. To the bowl with the coconut milk and vinegar, add the coconut nectar and vanilla. Whisk to combine.

5. Pour the wet ingredients into the flour mixture, and beat until a batter forms. Fold in the blueberries. Spoon the batter into the muffin liners, filling each one about three-quarters of the way full.

6. Bake for 20 to 24 minutes, until the tops are golden brown and a toothpick inserted in the center comes out clean. Allow the muffins to cool in the muffin tin for 20 to 30 minutes before transferring to a wire rack to cool completely, about 1 hour.

Storage: Place the muffins in an airtight container; loosely cover with aluminum foil, and store at room temperature for up to 2 days; or wrap individual muffins tightly in plastic wrap to store for up to 4 days. You can also keep them in the refrigerator for up to 5 days, but I suggest reheating before serving.

Ingredient tip: If you use frozen blueberries, I highly suggest thawing them beforehand, as stated in the recipe. Otherwise, the bake time and texture may vary, as frozen blueberries will "melt" in the baking process and release more moisture.

Pumpkin Muffins with Ginger-Vanilla Icing

PREP AHEAD • SOY-FREE | **Makes:** 10 muffins

Prep time: 20 minutes | **Cook time:** 25 minutes | **Cooling time:** 1 hour 5 minutes
Equipment: Box grater, muffin tin, hand mixer or stand mixer

I absolutely love the flavors found in a pumpkin muffin. I think the combination is one of my favorites when it comes to a baked good: The trifecta of cinnamon, allspice, and cloves simply tastes like fall—because the ginger is in the muffin and the icing, you get a sweet and spicy taste with each bite.

FOR THE MUFFINS

- ½ cup coconut sugar
- 1½ teaspoons grated peeled ginger (about a 1½-inch cube of ginger)
- ½ cup full-fat coconut milk or unsweetened almond milk
- 1 teaspoon apple cider vinegar
- 1 cup brown rice flour
- ¾ cup almond flour
- 2 tablespoons tapioca flour
- 2 teaspoons pumpkin pie spice (or 1 teaspoon ground cinnamon, ¼ teaspoon ground allspice, and ¼ teaspoon ground cloves)
- 1 teaspoon baking powder
- ½ teaspoon baking soda
- ¼ teaspoon sea salt
- ½ cup pumpkin purée
- 3 tablespoons maple syrup
- 1 teaspoon vanilla extract

1. Preheat the oven to 350°F. Line a muffin tin with muffin liners.

2. In a large bowl or stand mixer, combine the coconut sugar and ginger. Use your fingers to rub the mixture together until fragrant, 10 to 20 seconds.

3. In a medium bowl, combine the coconut milk and vinegar. Whisk and set aside.

4. To the bowl with the coconut sugar and ginger, add the brown rice flour, almond flour, tapioca flour, pumpkin pie spice, baking powder, baking soda, and salt. Stir to blend.

5. To the bowl with the coconut milk and vinegar, add the pumpkin purée, maple syrup, and vanilla. Whisk until creamy.

6. Pour the wet ingredients into the flour mixture, and beat until a batter forms. Spoon the batter into the muffin liners, filling each one about two-thirds to three-quarters of the way full.

1 cup coconut butter

3 tablespoons coconut oil

**1 teaspoon grated peeled
ginger (optional)**

1 teaspoon vanilla extract

7. Bake for 22 to 25 minutes, or until the tops are golden brown and a toothpick inserted in the center comes out clean. Allow the muffins to slightly cool, about 5 minutes, before transferring them to a wire rack to cool completely, about 1 hour.

8. To make the ginger-vanilla icing, in a small saucepan over low heat, combine the coconut butter and coconut oil. Heat until just melted together, 3 to 5 minutes, stirring frequently with a fork and breaking up any clumps. Add the ginger (if using) and whisk again. Remove from the heat and transfer to a small bowl. Allow to cool for 10 to 15 minutes, then add the vanilla and whisk. Spoon the icing over the cooled pumpkin muffins.

Storage: Place the muffins in an airtight container or loosely cover with aluminum foil, and store at room temperature for up to 2 days; or wrap individual plain muffins (not iced) tightly in plastic wrap, and store at room temperature for up to 4 days.

Vanilla Buckwheat Chia Granola

NUT-FREE • SOY-FREE | **Makes:** 4 cups [¼ cup = 1 serving]

Prep time: 10 minutes | **Cook time:** 25 minutes | **Cooling time:** 2 hours
Equipment: Baking sheet

Granola has always worn a halo of health in the nutrition world, but if you're not careful, you could be consuming a lot of sugar with each serving. The thought of making my own intimidated me for years until I realized how incredibly easy it is. Follow this recipe to a T or use it as a template, substituting various seeds or adding nuts to your liking. Sometimes I even like to add a teaspoon of cardamom for a subtle hint of something different. It might take some patience, but the longer you allow the granola to cool, the more clusters you will get. My favorite ways to enjoy this granola are mixed with almond milk or coconut yogurt, on top of a smoothie bowl, and by the handful for a quick, grab-and-go snack.

2½ cups gluten-free rolled oats

½ cup buckwheat groats

½ cup unsweetened coconut flakes

½ cup pumpkin seeds

½ cup sunflower seeds

¼ cup chia seeds

¼ teaspoon sea salt

1 tablespoon ground cinnamon

⅓ cup melted coconut oil or vegan butter

⅓ cup coconut nectar or maple syrup

1 teaspoon vanilla extract

1. Preheat the oven to 350°F. Line a baking sheet with parchment paper.

2. In a large bowl, combine the oats, buckwheat groats, coconut flakes, pumpkin seeds, sunflower seeds, chia seeds, salt, and cinnamon. Stir to blend.

3. In a medium bowl, whisk together the melted coconut oil, coconut nectar, and vanilla.

4. Pour the wet ingredients into the oat mixture. Use a spatula to mix until the dry ingredients are fully coated.

5. Transfer the granola mixture to the prepared baking sheet sheet and spread evenly, flattening with the spatula.

6. Bake for 15 minutes. Remove from the oven and press again with the spatula. Rotate the baking sheet to ensure even cooking. Bake for 7 to 10 more minutes, until the granola has turned slightly golden brown.

7. Allow the granola to completely cool on the baking sheet for 1 to 2 hours before breaking it up into clumps (the longer it cools, the more clumps you get).

Storage: Place the granola in an airtight container or zip-top bag in the pantry for up to 1 month.

Apple and Pear Crisp

PREP AHEAD • NUT-FREE • SOY-FREE | Serves: 10

Prep time: 20 minutes | **Cook time:** 45 minutes | **Cooling time:** 10 minutes
Equipment: 9-by-13-inch baking dish

This apple and pear crisp makes the perfect dish to feed a large crowd or prepare in advance for a busy workweek. Eat on its own or alongside your favorite dairy-free yogurt for a well-rounded morning meal. The buttery, cinnamon-sugar crumble makes it sweet enough to be disguised as dessert! Serve with some vegan ice cream or topped with coconut whipped cream (see Mississippi Mud Pie with Coconut Whipped Cream, page 154) for a post-dinner treat.

FOR THE FILLING

Nonstick cooking spray

4 cups thinly sliced pears (3 or 4 pears)

4 cups thinly sliced apples (3 or 4 apples)

Juice of ½ lemon

½ cup coconut sugar

¼ cup coconut flour

2 teaspoons ground cinnamon

1 teaspoon vanilla extract

½ teaspoon ground nutmeg

½ teaspoon ground cardamom

¼ teaspoon sea salt

FOR THE CRUMBLE TOPPING

1 cup gluten-free oats

½ cup coconut flour

⅓ cup coconut sugar

2 teaspoons ground cinnamon

¾ cup cold vegan butter, cut into 1-inch pieces

1. Preheat the oven to 350°F. Spray a 9-by-13-inch baking dish with cooking spray.

2. In a large bowl, combine the pears, apples, lemon juice, coconut sugar, coconut flour, cinnamon, vanilla, nutmeg, cardamom, and salt. Toss to coat. Transfer the apple-pear mixture to the prepared baking dish.

3. To make the crumble topping, in another large bowl, combine the oats, coconut flour, coconut sugar, and cinnamon. Stir until blended. Add the vegan butter, and use your hands to massage the butter into the oat mixture until a crumble forms. Sprinkle the crumble evenly over the apple-pear mixture.

4. Bake for 40 to 45 minutes, until the crumble turns golden brown and the apple-pear filling bubbles. Allow the crisp to cool slightly in the baking dish for 5 to 10 minutes. Serve warm.

Storage: Cover with aluminum foil, and store at room temperature for up to 2 days or in the refrigerator for up to 5 days. Enjoy it cold or reheat before serving.

Lemon Poppy Seed Muffins with Lemon Icing

PREP AHEAD • SOY-FREE | **Makes:** 10 to 12 muffins

Prep time: 15 minutes | **Cook time:** 25 minutes | **Cooling time:** 1 hour
Equipment: Box grater, muffin tin, hand mixer or stand mixer

There is something so sunny and delightful about a lemon poppy seed muffin. I find that rubbing the sugar and lemon zest together in the beginning makes the flavors meld beautifully and "pop" (pun intended) with each bite. Monk fruit is a melon native to Asia, and its extract has been used to sweeten foods for centuries. It works well with the lemon, but of course you can use any granulated sugar. These muffins have both a sweet flavor and a nutty texture, making them an uplifting breakfast option. If you want to increase the nutritional profile, substitute the poppy seeds with chia seeds.

FOR THE MUFFINS

½ cup monk fruit sweetener or granulated sugar

Grated zest of 1 lemon, divided (reserve 1 loosely packed teaspoon for the icing)

½ cup full-fat coconut milk or unsweetened almond milk

Juice of 1 lemon, divided (reserve 1 tablespoon for the icing)

1 cup almond flour

½ cup tapioca flour

⅓ cup brown rice flour

1 teaspoon baking powder

½ teaspoon baking soda

¼ teaspoon sea salt

¼ cup maple syrup

1 teaspoon vanilla extract

1 tablespoon poppy seeds

1. Preheat the oven to 350°F. Line a muffin tin with muffin liners.

2. In a large bowl or stand mixer, combine the monk fruit sweetener and the lemon zest. Rub the mixture together with your fingers until fragrant, 10 to 20 seconds.

3. In a medium bowl, whisk together the coconut milk and lemon juice. Set aside.

4. To the bowl with the monk fruit sweetener and zest, add the almond flour, tapioca flour, brown rice flour, baking powder, baking soda, and salt. Stir to blend.

5. To the bowl with the coconut milk and lemon juice, add the maple syrup and vanilla. Whisk to combine.

6. Pour the wet ingredients into the flour mixture, and beat until a batter forms. Fold in the poppy seeds. Spoon the batter into the muffin liners, filling each one about one-half to two-thirds of the way full.

(Continued)

FOR THE LEMON ICING

⅓ **cup coconut butter**

2 tablespoons coconut oil

1 teaspoon grated lemon zest

1 tablespoon lemon juice

½ **teaspoon vanilla extract**

7. Bake for 22 to 24 minutes, until a toothpick inserted in the center comes out clean. Immediately transfer the muffins to a wire rack to cool completely for at least 1 hour.

8. To make the lemon icing, in a small saucepan, combine the coconut butter and coconut oil, and heat over low heat. Stir frequently with a fork until just melted, 2 to 3 minutes, breaking up any clumps. Transfer the mixture to a small bowl and allow to slightly cool, about 10 minutes. Whisk in the lemon zest, lemon juice, and vanilla. Spoon 1 to 2 teaspoons of icing over each cooled muffin.

Storage: Loosely cover the muffins with aluminum foil or place in an airtight container, and store at room temperature for up to 3 days.

Morning Glory Muffins

OIL-FREE • PREP AHEAD • SOY-FREE | **Makes:** 12 muffins

Prep time: 25 minutes | **Cook time:** 25 minutes | **Cooling time:** 1 hour 5 minutes
Equipment: Box grater, muffin tin, hand mixer or stand mixer

I can see where morning glory muffins got their name! While the preparation might be a bit more laborious, it's worth it. The tartness of the apples, the sweetness of the carrots and raisins, and the nutty taste and texture of the walnuts and coconut marry perfectly with the spices to make for a glorious morning meal.

2 flax eggs (2 tablespoons ground flaxseed and 4 tablespoons water)

¾ cup unsweetened almond milk

1 teaspoon apple cider vinegar

¾ cup brown rice flour

¾ cup almond flour

½ cup coconut sugar

¼ cup gluten-free oat flour

2 teaspoons ground cinnamon

1½ teaspoons baking powder

1½ teaspoons grated peeled ginger

½ teaspoon baking soda

½ teaspoon ground nutmeg (optional)

¼ teaspoon sea salt

¼ cup maple syrup

1 apple, unpeeled, grated, and squeezed dry (about 1 cup)

1 cup grated carrots

¼ cup raisins

¼ cup chopped walnuts

¼ cup unsweetened coconut flakes

1. Preheat the oven to 350°F. Line a muffin tin with muffin liners.

2. In a small bowl, prepare the flax eggs by whisking together the ground flaxseed and water. Set aside for at least 10 minutes.

3. In a medium bowl, combine the almond milk and vinegar. Whisk and set aside.

4. In a large bowl or stand mixer, combine the brown rice flour, almond flour, coconut sugar, oat flour, cinnamon, baking powder, ginger, baking soda, nutmeg (if using), and salt. Stir to combine.

5. To the bowl with the almond milk and vinegar, add the flax eggs and maple syrup. Whisk.

6. Pour the wet ingredients into the flour mixture. Beat until a batter forms. Fold in the apple, carrots, raisins, walnuts, and coconut flakes.

7. Divide the batter among the muffin liners, filling each almost to the top. Bake for 22 to 24 minutes, until a toothpick inserted in the center comes out clean. Allow the muffins to slightly cool in the muffin tin, about 5 minutes, before transferring to a wire rack to cool completely for at least 1 hour.

Storage: Loosely cover the muffins with aluminum foil, and store at room temperature for up to 3 days; or store in an airtight container in the refrigerator for up to 5 days.

Cassava Biscuits

GRAIN-FREE • NUT-FREE • PREP AHEAD • SOY-FREE | **Makes:** 8 biscuits

Prep time: 20 minutes | **Cook time:** 20 minutes | **Cooling time:** 10 minutes
Equipment: Baking sheet, hand mixer or stand mixer, rolling pin
(optional), biscuit cutter or cookie cutter (optional)

Biscuits normally don't have a place in a gluten-free lifestyle—until now!
Cassava is a root vegetable native to South America, so it's not only naturally
grain-free but also a wonderful option for those who need a nut-free flour as
well. These biscuits are savory and crusty on the outside, soft and buttery on
the inside. Add a pat of your favorite vegan butter, or pair with blackberry-
chia jam (see Blackberry-Chia Jam Thumbprint Cookies, page 78).

⅔ cup full-fat coconut milk

1 teaspoon apple cider vinegar

1¾ cups cassava flour

1 tablespoon
    arrowroot starch

2 teaspoons baking powder

1 teaspoon sea salt

½ teaspoon baking soda

6 tablespoons vegan butter,
    at room temperature,
    plus more (optional)
    for spreading

1 tablespoon maple syrup

1. Preheat the oven to 425°F. Line a baking sheet with
parchment paper.

2. In a medium bowl, combine the coconut milk and vinegar.
Whisk and set aside.

3. In a large bowl or stand mixer, combine the cassava flour,
arrowroot starch, baking powder, salt, and baking soda. Stir
to blend.

4. Add 6 tablespoons of vegan butter to the flour mixture,
and use your hands to mix and massage the butter until a
crumbly dough forms.

5. To the bowl with the coconut milk and vinegar, add the
maple syrup. Whisk.

6. Pour the wet ingredients into the flour mixture, and beat until a batter forms. Use your hands to gather the dough into a ball, and allow the dough to rest for 5 to 10 minutes.

7. Place the ball of dough between two sheets of parchment paper, and using a rolling pin, roll the dough out to about 1 inch thick (no thinner!). Use a 2-inch to 3-inch biscuit cutter or small cookie cutter to cut 8 biscuits. Carefully place each biscuit on the prepared baking sheet. If you don't have a rolling pin or biscuit/cookie cutter, you can use your hands to form biscuits; just make sure they are at least 1 inch thick.

8. Thinly spread about ½ teaspoon vegan butter (if using) on top of each biscuit to add a golden color. Bake for 15 to 18 minutes, or until the outside looks crusty and the biscuits are slightly firm to the touch. Allow the biscuits to cool on the baking sheet for 5 to 10 minutes. Serve warm.

Storage: Wrap individual biscuits tightly in plastic wrap, and store at room temperature for up to 2 days. I suggest reheating before serving (both the oven and toaster oven work great).

Apple Cinnamon Donuts with Maple Glaze

PREP AHEAD • SOY-FREE | Makes: 6 to 8 donuts

Prep time: 20 minutes | **Cook time:** 20 minutes
Cooling time: 10 minutes (or 2 hours if glazing)
Equipment: One or two standard 6-cavity donut pans, hand mixer or stand mixer

Whenever I think of apple donuts, I imagine walking through a farmers' market in the fall with a cup of coffee or tea complementing each bite of the baked treat. These donuts are hearty yet moist, and the coconut butter topping offers extra flavor and an earthy sweetness.

FOR THE DONUTS

Nonstick cooking spray

¾ cup brown rice flour

½ cup almond flour

¼ cup tapioca flour

¼ cup coconut sugar

2 teaspoons ground cinnamon

½ teaspoon baking soda

¼ teaspoon ground nutmeg

¼ teaspoon sea salt

½ cup unsweetened almond milk or dairy-free milk

¼ cup unsweetened applesauce

¼ cup maple syrup

1 teaspoon vanilla extract

1 teaspoon apple cider vinegar

1. Preheat the oven to 350°F. Spray one or two standard 6-cavity donut pans with cooking spray.

2. In a large bowl or stand mixer, combine the brown rice flour, almond flour, tapioca flour, coconut sugar, cinnamon, baking soda, nutmeg, and salt. Stir to blend.

3. In a medium bowl, whisk together the almond milk, apple-sauce, maple syrup, vanilla, and vinegar.

4. Pour the wet ingredients into the flour mixture, and beat until a batter forms. Divide the batter evenly among the prepared donut pan cavities, filling each about three-quarters of the way full, and bake for 14 to 16 minutes, turning the pan halfway through to ensure even cooking. Allow the donuts to cool slightly in the pan, about 10 minutes, before carefully removing and transferring them to a wire rack or cutting board. Enjoy warm, or allow to completely cool for about 2 hours if glazing.

5. To make the maple glaze (if using), in a small saucepan over low heat, combine the coconut butter and coconut oil. Using a fork or wire whisk, stir frequently until the coconut oil melts and the coconut butter is creamy (about halfway melted, but there will still be some clumps), 1 to 2 minutes, watching carefully to make sure the mixture doesn't burn.

½ cup coconut butter

¼ cup coconut oil

1 tablespoon maple syrup

1 teaspoon ground cinnamon

1 teaspoon vanilla extract

Coconut sugar, for
   dusting (optional)

6. Remove from the heat and transfer the glaze to a small glass or ceramic bowl. Add the maple syrup, cinnamon, and vanilla. Stir vigorously with a wire whisk until creamy and thickened (if there are still some coconut butter clumps, that is fine). Use immediately.

7. Spoon the glaze over the donuts until it is used up. Dust with coconut sugar (if using).

Storage: Wrap individual donuts tightly in plastic wrap, and store at room temperature for up to 3 days.

Raspberry Scones

PREP AHEAD • SOY-FREE | **Makes:** 6 scones

Prep time: 25 minutes, plus 2 hours 5 minutes to chill
Cook time: 20 minutes | **Cooling time:** 2 hours
Equipment: Hand mixer or stand mixer, baking sheet

Not to be confused with biscuits, scones have a special texture: light and fluffy on the inside with a slightly crispy crust. Raspberries' natural sweetness blends perfectly with the buttery taste that surrounds them in this recipe. I love these scones drizzled with a bit of melted coconut butter.

2 flax eggs (2 tablespoons ground flaxseed and 4 tablespoons water)

¼ cup full-fat coconut milk

½ teaspoon apple cider vinegar

¾ cup brown rice flour

¾ cup almond flour

⅓ cup coconut sugar or granulated sugar

1 teaspoon baking powder

½ teaspoon baking soda

¼ teaspoon sea salt

6 tablespoons cold vegan butter, cut into 1-inch pieces

1 tablespoon maple syrup

1 teaspoon vanilla extract

2 tablespoons melted coconut oil

½ cup fresh raspberries or fresh berries of choice

Nonstick cooking spray

1. In a small bowl, prepare the flax eggs by whisking together the ground flaxseed and water. Set aside for at least 10 minutes.

2. In a small bowl, whisk together the coconut milk and vinegar. Set aside.

3. In a large bowl or stand mixer, combine the brown rice flour, almond flour, coconut sugar, baking powder, baking soda, and salt. Stir to blend.

4. Add the vegan butter to the flour mixture, and use your hands to mix and massage it until a crumbly dough forms.

5. To the bowl with the coconut milk and vinegar, whisk in the maple syrup and vanilla.

6. Pour the coconut milk mixture, as well as the flax eggs, into the bowl with the mixture flour mixture. While beating on low speed, incorporate the melted coconut oil, and continue to beat until a thick dough forms (slightly increasing the speed if you need to; just be careful not to overbeat). Add the raspberries, and beat again on low speed or fold them in by hand until incorporated. Gather the dough into a ball with your hands, and wrap it tightly in plastic wrap. Refrigerate for 2 hours.

7. Preheat the oven to 425°F. Line a baking sheet with parchment paper.

8. Transfer the dough to the prepared baking sheet, and use your hands to shape it into a 1½-inch-thick circle. Use a large knife sprayed with cooking spray to cut the dough like a pizza into six triangles of the same size. Keeping them close together (almost touching), use the knife or a spatula sprayed with cooking spray to separate each scone by about ⅛ inch. Transfer the baking sheet to the freezer for 5 minutes.

9. Bake for 10 minutes, then loosely cover with aluminum foil, and bake for 10 more minutes. Allow the scones to completely cool for at least 2 hours on the baking sheet.

Storage: I suggest enjoying these scones on the day they are baked; otherwise, wrap individual scones tightly in plastic wrap, and store at room temperature until the next day.

Ingredient tip: I highly recommend using fresh berries, as frozen berries will affect the texture and ability of the scones to rise.

Streusel Coffee Cake

NUT-FREE OPTION • PREP AHEAD • SOY-FREE | Serves: 9

Prep time: 20 minutes | **Cook time:** 45 minutes | **Cooling time:** 1 hour
Equipment: 8-by-8-inch baking dish, hand mixer or stand mixer

There are a couple of ways to make a coffee cake, but the components
I believe to be the most delicious are a "buttery" crumble topping
with a cinnamon-sugar center. A delightfully sweet experience with
each bite that you can enjoy at any age on any morning!

FOR THE CAKE

2 flax eggs (2 tablespoons
  ground flaxseed and
  4 tablespoons water)

1 cup full-fat coconut milk or
  unsweetened almond milk

1 teaspoon apple cider vinegar

1¼ cups brown rice flour

¾ cup almond flour or all-
  purpose gluten-free flour

⅓ cup coconut sugar

3 tablespoons tapioca flour

2 teaspoons ground
  cinnamon

1½ teaspoons baking powder

½ teaspoon baking soda

¼ teaspoon sea salt

2 tablespoons maple syrup

1 teaspoon vanilla extract

2 tablespoons melted
  coconut oil

1. Preheat the oven to 350°F. Line an 8-by-8-inch baking
dish with parchment paper.

2. In a small bowl, prepare the flax eggs by whisking together
the ground flaxseed and water. Set aside for at least
10 minutes.

3. In a medium bowl, whisk together the coconut milk and
vinegar. Set aside.

4. In a large bowl or stand mixer, combine the brown rice
flour, almond flour, coconut sugar, tapioca flour, cinnamon,
baking powder, baking soda, and salt. Stir to blend.

5. To make the crumble topping, in a separate medium bowl,
combine the almond flour, coconut sugar, and cinnamon.
Stir. Add the vegan butter, and use your hands to mix and
massage it into the flour until a crumble forms. Refrigerate
until ready to use.

6. To make the center filling, in a small bowl, combine the
coconut sugar and cinnamon. Pour in the melted vegan
butter, and stir to blend. Set aside.

7. To the bowl with the milk and apple cider vinegar, add the
flax eggs, maple syrup, and vanilla. Whisk. Add the melted
coconut oil, and whisk again.

1 cup almond flour or all-
purpose gluten-free flour

¼ cup coconut sugar

1 teaspoon ground cinnamon

4 to 5 tablespoons cold
vegan butter, cut
into 1-inch pieces

¾ cup coconut sugar

1 tablespoon ground
cinnamon

3 tablespoons melted vegan
butter or coconut oil

8. Pour the wet ingredients into the flour mixture, and beat until a batter forms. Using a spatula, transfer half of the batter into the bottom of the prepared baking dish. Sprinkle the center filling evenly on top. Add the rest of the batter, wetting the spatula to evenly spread, as the batter will be somewhat thick. Sprinkle the crumble on top.

9. Bake for 40 to 45 minutes, until a toothpick inserted in the center comes out clean. Allow the cake to completely cool in the baking dish for at least 1 hour before slicing and serving.

Storage: Cover the cake loosely with aluminum foil in the baking dish, and store at room temperature for up to 4 days.

Serving tip: You can serve the cake warm, but it might fall apart if you don't allow it to completely cool.

Sticky Buns

GRAIN-FREE • PREP AHEAD • SOY-FREE | **Makes:** 6 buns

Prep time: 20 minutes, plus 1 hour to chill
Cook time: 30 minutes | **Cooling time:** 10 minutes
Equipment: Hand mixer or stand mixer, 8-by-8-inch or
9-inch round baking dish, rolling pin

The first time I hosted Christmas at my house, I started a new tradition: sticky buns for breakfast! For years to come, I would imagine waking up while everyone else was still asleep, basking in the stillness of my surroundings, and having these buns ready to serve to loved ones.

FOR THE DOUGH

3 cups almond flour

½ cup tapioca flour or arrowroot starch

⅓ cup coconut sugar

2 teaspoons ground cinnamon

1 teaspoon baking powder

½ teaspoon baking soda

¼ teaspoon sea salt

⅓ cup melted vegan butter or coconut oil

¼ cup unsweetened almond milk or dairy-free milk of choice

¼ cup maple syrup

1 teaspoon apple cider vinegar

1 teaspoon vanilla extract

Nonstick cooking spray

1. In a large bowl or stand mixer, combine the almond flour, tapioca flour, coconut sugar, cinnamon, baking powder, baking soda, and salt. Stir to blend.

2. In a medium bowl, whisk together the melted vegan butter, almond milk, maple syrup, vinegar, and vanilla.

3. Pour the wet ingredients into the flour mixture, and beat until a dough forms. Gather the dough in a ball, and wrap tightly in plastic wrap. Refrigerate for 1 hour.

4. Meanwhile, to make the filling, in a small bowl, mix the chopped raisins and dates. Pour in the melted vegan butter, and stir to coat. Add the coconut sugar and cinnamon, and stir until mixed well. Set aside.

5. Preheat the oven to 350°F. Lightly spray an 8-by-8-inch or 9-inch round baking dish with cooking spray.

6. Place the ball of dough between two sheets of parchment paper. Using a rolling pin, roll the dough out until ½ inch thick and 10 to 12 inches in diameter. Spoon the filling onto the dough and spread evenly toward the edges. Using your hands, roll up the dough into a log (lift the bottom piece of parchment paper to help get it started). Use a knife sprayed with cooking spray to cut the log of dough into 1½-inch to 2-inch pieces to form the buns.

FOR THE FILLING

¼ cup chopped raisins

4 pitted and chopped
  Medjool dates (or 2 to
  3 tablespoons raisins)

¼ cup melted vegan
  butter or coconut oil

3 tablespoons coconut sugar

2 teaspoons ground
  cinnamon

FOR THE FROSTING

⅓ cup coconut oil

⅓ cup vegan butter

3 tablespoons vegan
  cream cheese, at
  room temperature

2 tablespoons coconut sugar

1 tablespoon maple syrup

1 teaspoon vanilla extract

7. Place the buns in the prepared baking dish side by side so that they are touching. Bake for 27 to 30 minutes, until golden brown and firm to the touch.

8. To make the frosting, in a large bowl, mix the coconut oil, vegan butter, and vegan cream cheese. Beat until fluffy, about 30 seconds. Add the coconut sugar and beat again. Add the maple syrup and vanilla extract, and beat until mixed well.

9. Allow the buns to slightly cool in the baking dish, about 10 minutes. Use a knife to separate each bun. Spread the frosting evenly on top, either while in the baking dish or once plated. Serve warm.

Storage: Cover loosely with aluminum foil, and store at room temperature for up to 3 days or refrigerate for up to 5 days. The frosting will harden when cold, so allow the buns to sit at room temperature for 20 minutes, or warm before eating.

Plan-ahead tip: The dough can be made 1 to 2 days in advance. Keep wrapped in plastic wrap in the refrigerator. Buns can also be prepared up to 4 months in advance. Follow the instructions through step 6, wrap each one tightly in plastic wrap, and transfer to the freezer. When ready to use, thaw overnight in the refrigerator, then place each bun in the baking dish and bake as stated.

Orange-Cranberry Bread, page 50

BREADS

Cornbread

NUT-FREE OPTION • SOY-FREE | Serves: 9

Prep time: 15 minutes | **Cook time:** 30 minutes | **Cooling time:** 1 hour
Equipment: 8-by-8-inch baking dish, hand mixer or stand mixer

As a Southern girl, I love a piece of fluffy cornbread. The beautiful thing about it is that it can be consumed during any season. Serve it as a side during a summer dinner, or pair it with your favorite bean chili in the winter. (In fact, I don't believe in eating chili without it!) If you love a cornbread that is sweet and soft, this is the recipe for you!

2 flax eggs (2 tablespoons ground flaxseed and 4 tablespoons water)

¾ cup full-fat coconut milk or unsweetened almond milk

1 teaspoon apple cider vinegar

1 cup cornmeal

½ cup brown rice flour or all-purpose gluten-free flour

½ cup almond flour or additional ½ cup brown rice flour

⅓ cup coconut sugar

1½ teaspoons baking powder

½ teaspoon baking soda

¼ teaspoon sea salt

2 tablespoons melted coconut oil

2 tablespoons maple syrup or coconut nectar

1. Preheat the oven to 350°F. Line an 8-by-8-inch baking dish with parchment paper.

2. In a small bowl, prepare the flax eggs by whisking together the ground flaxseed and water. Set aside for at least 10 minutes.

3. In a separate small bowl, combine the coconut milk and vinegar. Whisk and set aside.

4. In a large bowl or stand mixer, mix the cornmeal, brown rice flour, almond flour, coconut sugar, baking powder, baking soda, and salt. Stir to combine.

5. To the bowl with the coconut milk and vinegar, add the flax eggs, melted coconut oil, and maple syrup. Whisk until creamy.

6. Pour the wet ingredients into the flour mixture, and beat until a batter forms. Transfer the batter to the prepared baking dish.

7. Bake for 27 to 30 minutes, until golden brown and a toothpick inserted in the center comes out clean. Allow the cornbread to completely cool in the baking dish for at least 1 hour.

Storage: Cover with aluminum foil, and store at room temperature for up to 3 days.

Gingerbread

Prep time: 20 minutes | **Cook time:** 30 minutes | **Cooling time:** 1 hour
Equipment: Box grater, 8-by-8-inch baking dish, hand mixer or stand mixer

Whether in Grain-Free Gingerbread Men (page 80) or in this easy baked bread, the spicy sweetness of these ingredients is sure to bring a smile to your face. The flavor combination is one of a kind, and I hope each bite fills you with holiday spirit. Pair it with your morning cup of coffee for breakfast or with hot chocolate for dessert—you really can't go wrong!

2 flax eggs (2 tablespoons ground flaxseed and 4 tablespoons water)

1 cup brown rice flour or all-purpose gluten-free flour

1 cup almond flour or 1 cup more brown rice flour or all-purpose gluten-free flour

⅓ cup coconut sugar

2 tablespoons tapioca flour (omit if using all-purpose gluten-free flour)

2 teaspoons grated peeled ginger

1½ teaspoons baking powder

1 teaspoon ground cinnamon

½ teaspoon baking soda

½ teaspoon ground cloves

½ teaspoon ground allspice

¼ teaspoon sea salt

¾ cup full-fat coconut milk or unsweetened almond milk

¼ cup blackstrap molasses

1. Preheat the oven to 350°F. Line an 8-by-8-inch baking dish with parchment paper.

2. In a medium bowl, prepare the flax eggs by whisking together the ground flaxseed and water. Set aside for at least 10 minutes.

3. In a large bowl or stand mixer, mix the brown rice flour, almond flour, coconut sugar, tapioca flour, ginger, baking powder, cinnamon, baking soda, cloves, allspice, and salt. Stir to blend.

4. In the bowl with the flax eggs, whisk the coconut milk and molasses.

5. Pour the wet ingredients into the flour mixture. Beat until a batter forms.

6. Transfer the batter to the prepared baking dish. Bake for 27 to 30 minutes, until a toothpick inserted in the center comes out clean. Allow the bread to completely cool in the baking dish for at least 1 hour.

Storage: Cover with aluminum foil, and store at room temperature for up to 3 days.

Sliced Sandwich Bread

NUT-FREE • PREP AHEAD • SOY-FREE | **Makes:** 1 loaf (10 slices)

Prep time: 10 minutes, plus 30 minutes to rise
Cook time: 55 minutes | **Cooling time:** 2 hours 5 minutes
Equipment: 8½-by-4½-inch or 9-by-5-inch loaf pan, hand
mixer or stand mixer, food thermometer (optional)

The sandwich just so happens to be one of the easiest, most portable meals to throw together. Therefore, I can completely understand the worry when one goes gluten-free and immediately associates it with going sandwich-free. This doesn't have to be the case! While there are store-bought options out there, many are filled with gums, refined sugars, and starches that don't always agree with people either. Use this recipe when you want to have sliced bread on hand. It is so easy to make and tastes good too.

1½ cups warm water

3 tablespoons maple syrup

1 (¼-ounce) packet
   dry active yeast

1½ cups brown rice flour

1½ cups all-purpose
   gluten-free flour

1 tablespoon baking powder

1 teaspoon sea salt

¼ cup extra-virgin olive oil

2 teaspoons apple
   cider vinegar

1. Line a 8½-by-4½-inch or 9-by-5-inch loaf pan with parchment paper.

2. In a small bowl or 1-quart measuring cup, combine the warm water and maple syrup. Stir in the yeast until dissolved, and set aside for 10 minutes.

3. In a large bowl or stand mixer, mix the brown rice flour, gluten-free flour, baking powder, and salt. Stir to blend.

4. Add the proofed yeast to the bowl with the flour mixture. While beating on low speed, slowly incorporate the olive oil, then the apple cider vinegar. Continue to beat until a batter forms (but be careful not to overbeat).

5. Transfer the batter to the prepared loaf pan. Allow the bread to rise for 30 minutes.

6. Meanwhile, preheat the oven to 375°F.

7. Bake for 45 minutes. Cover the bread with aluminum foil, and bake for another 7 to 10 minutes, until the top turns golden brown or the internal temperature reaches between 200°F and 210°F. Allow the bread to cool in the pan for 5 minutes, then remove (pan and bread will be hot!) and transfer to a wire rack to cool completely, about 2 hours. Use a sharp knife to slice and serve.

Storage: Wrap individual slices in aluminum foil or plastic wrap, and store at room temperature for up to 5 days. Bread will also keep frozen for up to 3 months. Wrap individual slices in plastic wrap before freezing.

Butternut Brown Bread

PREP AHEAD • SOY-FREE | **Makes:** 1 loaf (10 slices)

Prep time: 15 minutes, plus 30 minutes to rest
Cook time: 1 hour 5 minutes | **Cooling time:** 2 hours 10 minutes
Equipment: Hand mixer or stand mixer, 8½-by-4½-inch or
9-by-5-inch loaf pan, food thermometer (optional)

There is a charming corner café a couple of blocks from my house. Upon being seated, they serve the softest, sweetest brown bread. Given that my gluten-free lifestyle no longer allows me to partake in this particular bread, it is the inspiration behind this recipe. Not only is it just as delicious, but knowing it aligns with my dietary needs makes it that much more pleasurable to eat.

2 flax eggs (2 tablespoons ground flaxseed and 4 tablespoons water)

1¼ cups brown rice flour

1 cup almond flour

¾ cup coconut sugar

3 tablespoons tapioca flour

1½ teaspoons baking powder

1 teaspoon ground cinnamon

½ teaspoon baking soda

¼ teaspoon sea salt

1 cup butternut squash purée

¼ cup maple syrup

⅓ cup melted vegan butter

1 teaspoon vanilla extract

1 teaspoon apple cider vinegar

1. In a medium bowl, prepare the flax eggs by whisking together the ground flaxseed and water. Set aside for at least 10 minutes.

2. In a large bowl or stand mixer, mix the brown rice flour, almond flour, coconut sugar, tapioca flour, baking powder, cinnamon, baking soda, and salt. Stir to blend.

3. To the bowl with the flax eggs, add the butternut squash purée, maple syrup, melted vegan butter, vanilla, and vinegar. Whisk until creamy.

4. Pour the wet ingredients into the flour mixture, and beat until a batter forms. If needed, mix the batter with a spatula. Let the batter rest in the bowl at room temperature for 30 minutes.

5. Meanwhile, preheat the oven to 350°F. Line a 8½-by-4½-inch or 9-by-5-inch loaf pan with parchment paper.

6. Transfer the batter to the prepared loaf pan. Bake for 45 to 50 minutes, then cover with aluminum foil. Increase the oven temperature to 400°F. Bake for 15 more minutes, until golden brown and a toothpick inserted in the center comes out clean or the internal temperature reaches between 190°F and 200°F. Allow the bread to cool in the pan for 10 minutes before carefully removing and transferring to a wire rack to cool completely, at least 2 hours.

Storage: Wrap the loaf or individual slices in plastic wrap, and store at room temperature for up to 5 days.

Ingredient tip: For easy preparation, use butternut squash purée from a can. You can also substitute with pumpkin purée or sweet potato purée.

Pumpkin Bread

PREP AHEAD • SOY-FREE | **Makes:** 1 loaf (10 slices)

Prep time: 15 minutes, plus 20 minutes to rest
Cook time: 55 minutes | **Cooling time:** 2 hours
Equipment: Hand mixer or stand mixer, 8½-by-4½-inch or
9-by-5-inch loaf pan, food thermometer (optional)

As soon as fall rolls around, pumpkin gets incorporated into everything: breakfast, drinks, and desserts, to name a few. I love this bread, which makes a great base for spreads (like almond butter, coconut butter, or vegan butter). Enjoy a slice as a satiating snack or as part of a meal (as a side to a hearty soup comes to mind).

2 flax eggs (2 tablespoons ground flaxseed and 4 tablespoons water)

1¼ cups brown rice flour

1 cup almond flour

⅓ cup coconut sugar

¼ cup tapioca flour

2 teaspoons pumpkin pie spice (or 1 teaspoon ground cinnamon, ½ teaspoon ground ginger, ¼ teaspoon ground allspice, and ¼ teaspoon ground nutmeg)

1½ teaspoons baking powder

½ teaspoon ground cinnamon

½ teaspoon baking soda

¼ teaspoon sea salt

1 cup pumpkin purée

¼ cup maple syrup

1 teaspoon apple cider vinegar

1 teaspoon vanilla extract

¼ cup melted coconut oil

1. In a medium bowl, prepare the flax eggs by whisking together the ground flaxseed and water. Set aside for at least 10 minutes.

2. In a large bowl or stand mixer, mix the brown rice flour, almond flour, coconut sugar, tapioca flour, pumpkin pie spice, baking powder, cinnamon, baking soda, and salt. Stir to blend.

3. In the bowl with the flax eggs, add the pumpkin purée, maple syrup, vinegar, and vanilla. Whisk until creamy. Add the melted coconut oil, and whisk again.

4. Pour the wet ingredients into the flour mixture, and beat until a batter forms. Allow the batter to rest in the bowl at room temperature for 20 minutes.

5. Meanwhile, preheat the oven to 350°F. Line a 8½-by-4½-inch or 9-by-5-inch loaf pan with parchment paper.

6. Using a spatula, mix the batter a few times, and transfer to the prepared loaf pan. Bake for 40 minutes. Cover with aluminum foil and bake for another 10 to 15 minutes, until a toothpick inserted in the center comes out clean or the internal temperature reaches between 190°F and 200°F. Allow the bread to completely cool in the baking dish, at least 2 hours.

Storage: Wrap the loaf or individual slices in plastic wrap, and store at room temperature for up to 4 days.

Apple-Oat Bread

NUT-FREE • PREP AHEAD • SOY-FREE | **Makes:** 1 loaf (10 slices)

Prep time: 20 minutes | **Cook time:** 1 hour | **Cooling time:** 2 hours 10 minutes
Equipment: Box grater, 8½-by-4½-inch or 9-by-5-inch loaf pan,
hand mixer or stand mixer, food thermometer (optional)

What I love best about this bread is the crumb when you cut into it. The oats provide a dense texture, yet the center is still soft and moist thanks to the fresh fruit found inside. Hearty and slightly sweet, this bread pairs perfectly with your favorite nut butter and some extra cinnamon for sprinkling, but it's also enjoyable enough on its own.

2 flax eggs (2 tablespoons ground flaxseed and 4 tablespoons water)

1¼ cups brown rice flour

½ cup gluten-free oat flour

½ cup gluten-free oats

⅓ cup coconut sugar

2 tablespoons tapioca flour

1 tablespoon apple pie spice (or 1½ teaspoons ground cinnamon, ¾ teaspoon ground nutmeg, ½ teaspoon ground allspice, and ¼ teaspoon ground cardamom)

1½ teaspoons baking powder

½ teaspoon baking soda

¼ teaspoon sea salt

¾ cup unsweetened applesauce

⅓ cup maple syrup

1 teaspoon apple cider vinegar

1 teaspoon vanilla extract

¼ cup melted coconut oil

1 cup grated apple (from 2 small apples), squeezed dry

1. Preheat the oven to 350°F. Line a 8½-by-4½-inch or 9-by-5-inch loaf pan with parchment paper.

2. In a medium bowl, prepare the flax eggs by whisking together the ground flaxseed and water. Set aside for at least 10 minutes.

3. In a large bowl or stand mixer, mix the brown rice flour, oat flour, oats, coconut sugar, tapioca flour, apple pie spice, baking powder, baking soda, and salt. Stir to blend.

4. To the bowl with the flax eggs, add the applesauce, maple syrup, vinegar, and vanilla. Whisk until creamy.

5. Pour the wet ingredients into the flour mixture, and while beating on medium speed, slowly incorporate the melted coconut oil, and continue to beat until a batter forms, increasing the speed as you need to. Fold in the grated apple.

6. Transfer the batter to the prepared loaf pan, and bake for 50 minutes to 1 hour, until a toothpick inserted in the center comes out clean or the internal temperature reaches between 190°F and 200°F. Allow the bread to slightly cool in the loaf pan, about 10 minutes, before carefully removing and transferring to a wire rack to cool completely, about 2 hours.

Storage: Wrap the loaf or individual slices in plastic wrap, and store at room temperature for up to 4 days.

Blueberry-Lemon Bread

PREP AHEAD • SOY-FREE | **Makes:** 1 loaf (10 slices)

Prep time: 20 minutes, plus 20 minutes to rest
Cook time: 1 hour | **Cooling time:** 2 hours
Equipment: Box grater, hand mixer or stand mixer, 8½-by-4½-inch
or 9-by-5-inch loaf pan, food thermometer (optional)

Fair warning: This bread could be confused as cake! The bread is sweet
and moist, with the berry and citrus flavors coming together deliciously in
every slice. It's perfect to serve at an Easter brunch or a summer luncheon,
or simply to have on hand for a feel-good breakfast or healthy dessert.
If you ever find yourself wondering what to do with the blueberries you
bought at the store or farmers' market, this bread is an amazing option!

FOR THE BREAD

- ½ cup coconut sugar or monk fruit sweetener
- 1 tablespoon grated lemon zest (from about 1 large or 2 small lemons)
- 1½ cups brown rice flour
- ½ cup almond flour
- 2 tablespoons tapioca flour
- 1½ teaspoons baking powder
- ½ teaspoon baking soda
- ¼ teaspoon sea salt
- ½ cup full-fat coconut milk or unsweetened almond milk
- ¼ cup freshly squeezed lemon juice (from about 1 large or 2 small lemons)
- ¼ cup maple syrup
- 2 tablespoons unsweetened applesauce
- 1 teaspoon vanilla extract
- ¾ cup fresh blueberries

1. In a large bowl or stand mixer, combine the coconut sugar and lemon zest. Massage together with your fingers until fragrant, 20 to 30 seconds. Add the brown rice flour, almond flour, tapioca flour, baking powder, baking soda, and salt. Stir to blend.

2. In a medium bowl, combine the coconut milk, lemon juice, maple syrup, applesauce, and vanilla. Whisk until creamy.

3. Pour the wet ingredients into the flour mixture. Beat until a batter forms. Fold in the blueberries. Let the batter rest in the bowl at room temperature for 20 minutes.

4. Meanwhile, preheat the oven to 350°F. Line a 8½-by-4½-inch or 9-by-5-inch loaf pan with parchment paper.

5. Mix the batter with a spatula, then transfer the batter to the prepared loaf pan. Bake for 55 minutes to 1 hour, until a toothpick inserted in the center comes out clean or the internal temperature reaches between 200°F and 205°F. Allow the bread to completely cool in the loaf pan, at least 2 hours.

⅓ cup coconut butter

2 tablespoons coconut oil

1 teaspoon grated lemon zest

1 tablespoon freshly
squeezed lemon juice

½ teaspoon vanilla extract

6. To make the lemon icing (if using), in a small saucepan, combine the coconut butter and coconut oil, and heat over low heat. Stir frequently with a fork until just melted, 2 to 3 minutes, breaking up any clumps. Transfer the mixture to a separate small bowl, and allow to slightly cool, about 10 minutes. Whisk in the lemon zest, lemon juice, and vanilla. Spoon the icing on top of the cooled bread.

Storage: Wrap individual slices in plastic wrap, and store at room temperature for up to 4 days or in the refrigerator for up to 1 week.

Ingredient tip: You can use the same lemon(s) for both the zest and juice, but be sure to zest the lemon(s) before juicing. To more easily squeeze the juice from the lemons, roll them on the countertop, applying pressure as you do. Use a citrus press, or loosen the flesh of the lemon with a fork before squeezing.

Italian-Style Flatbread

GRAIN-FREE OPTION • NUT-FREE • SOY-FREE | **Makes:** 1 flatbread

Prep time: 10 minutes | **Cook time:** 25 minutes
Equipment: 12-inch oven-safe skillet, hand mixer or stand mixer

One of the most frequently asked questions I receive when it comes to transitioning to a gluten-free way of eating is about pizza. I am here to set the record straight: You do not need to live life without pizza! I love this flatbread as an option, which uses either chickpea flour or brown rice flour and some savory spices as a base for your toppings of choice. This recipe results in a thin, crispy crust, but feel free to double the ingredients if you want a thicker crust (just know you will have to adjust the cook time accordingly). I have also used this flatbread for avocado and hummus toast.

Nonstick cooking spray

1 cup chickpea flour (also called garbanzo bean flour) or brown rice flour

1 tablespoon Italian seasoning blend (or ½ teaspoon dried basil, ½ teaspoon dried oregano, ½ teaspoon parsley flakes, ½ teaspoon sea salt, ½ teaspoon dried rosemary, ¼ teaspoon garlic powder, and ¼ teaspoon onion powder)

½ cup plus 2 tablespoons water

2 tablespoons extra-virgin olive oil

1. Preheat the oven to 425°F. Spray the bottom of a 12-inch oven-safe skillet with cooking spray, or line the bottom with parchment paper.

2. In a large bowl or stand mixer, mix the chickpea flour and Italian seasoning. Stir to blend.

3. While slowly whisking by hand or beating on low speed, gradually add the water, then the olive oil, until a batter forms (the consistency should be similar to a thick pancake batter).

4. Transfer the batter to the prepared skillet, and use a spatula to evenly spread across the bottom. Bake for 20 minutes, until the edges look crispy and have started to pull away from the side of the skillet. Reduce the oven temperature to 400°F, add toppings, if desired (like vegetables or cooked meat), while the flatbread is still hot in the skillet. Cook for 10 to 12 more minutes, until everything is heated through.

Storage: Wrap the bread in aluminum foil, and store in the refrigerator for up to 5 days.

Chocolate Loaf

PREP AHEAD • SOY-FREE | **Makes:** 1 loaf (10 slices)

Prep time: 10 minutes, plus 20 minutes to rest
Cook time: 1 hour 10 minutes | **Cooling time:** 2 hours
Equipment: Hand mixer or stand mixer, high-speed blender or food processor (optional), 8½-by-4½-inch or 9-by-5-inch loaf pan, food thermometer (optional)

Apparently, chocolate bread is a thing, and thank goodness for that! I love this loaf as a sweet treat or even as an energizing snack. The avocado coupled with the full-fat coconut milk provides that plant-based buttery feel that is melt-in-your-mouth amazing! I recommend using Enjoy Life brand dairy-free chocolate chips.

1 cup brown rice flour

¾ cup almond flour

½ cup unsweetened cocoa powder

½ cup coconut sugar

2 tablespoons tapioca flour

1½ teaspoons baking powder

½ teaspoon baking soda

¼ teaspoon sea salt

½ cup full-fat coconut milk

1 ripe avocado, mashed

⅓ cup maple syrup

2 teaspoons vanilla extract

¼ cup melted coconut oil

½ cup dairy-free chocolate chips, plus more for topping, if desired

1. In a large bowl or stand mixer, combine the brown rice flour, almond flour, cocoa powder, coconut sugar, tapioca flour, baking powder, baking soda, and salt. Stir to blend.

2. In a medium bowl or using a high-speed blender or food processor, combine the coconut milk, avocado, maple syrup, and vanilla. Whisk or blend until creamy.

3. Pour the wet ingredients into the flour mixture. While beating on low speed, slowly incorporate the melted coconut oil, and continue to beat until a batter forms, increasing the speed as needed. Fold in the chocolate chips, and allow the batter to rest in the bowl at room temperature for 20 minutes.

4. Meanwhile, preheat the oven to 350°F. Line a 8½-by-4½-inch or 9-by-5-inch loaf pan with parchment paper.

5. Using a spatula, mix the batter and transfer it to the prepared loaf pan. Sprinkle more chocolate chips on top, if desired. Bake for 1 hour to 1 hour 10 minutes, until a toothpick inserted in the center comes out clean or the internal temperature reaches 190°F. Allow the bread to cool for 1 hour in the loaf pan before removing and transferring to a wire rack to cool for another hour.

Storage: Wrap the loaf or individual slices in plastic wrap, and store at room temperature for up to 5 days.

Chai-Spiced Pear Bread

NUT-FREE • OIL-FREE • PREP AHEAD • SOY-FREE | **Makes:** 1 loaf (10 slices)

Prep time: 20 minutes, plus 20 minutes to rest
Cook time: 1 hour | **Cooling time:** 2 hours 10 minutes
Equipment: Food processor, hand mixer or stand mixer,
8½-by-4½-inch or 9-by-5-inch loaf pan, food thermometer (optional)

The flavor combination of pear and chai sounds exotic, but it is likely that you have the spices already on hand. I urge you to give it a try and feel the warming and grounding effects of each bite. Pear purée works great in vegan baking, providing a softer texture without being overwhelmingly fruity.

2 flax eggs (2 tablespoons ground flaxseed and 4 tablespoons water)
1¼ cups brown rice flour
¾ cup gluten-free oat flour
⅓ cup coconut sugar
2 tablespoons tapioca flour
2 teaspoons ground ginger
1½ teaspoons ground cinnamon
1½ teaspoons baking powder
½ teaspoon ground cardamom
½ teaspoon ground allspice
½ teaspoon baking soda
¼ teaspoon ground cloves
¼ teaspoon sea salt
1 cup pear purée (from 2 medium pears blended in a food processor— I use Bartlett pears)
⅓ cup maple syrup
1 teaspoon apple cider vinegar
1 teaspoon vanilla extract

1. In a medium bowl, prepare the flax eggs by whisking together the ground flaxseed and water. Set aside for 10 minutes.

2. In a large bowl or stand mixer, combine the brown rice flour, oat flour, coconut sugar, tapioca flour, ginger, cinnamon, baking powder, cardamom, allspice, baking soda, cloves, and salt. Stir to blend.

3. To the bowl with the flax eggs, add the pear purée, maple syrup, vinegar, and vanilla. Whisk until creamy.

4. Pour the wet ingredients into the flour mixture. Beat until a batter forms, using a spatula to scrape down the sides of the bowl as needed to make sure everything blends together. Allow the batter to rest in the bowl at room temperature for 20 minutes.

5. Meanwhile, preheat the oven to 350°F. Line a 8½-by-4½-inch or 9-by-5-inch loaf pan with parchment paper.

6. Mix the batter once more with a spatula, and transfer the batter to the prepared loaf pan. Bake for 45 minutes. Cover the loaf pan with aluminum foil, and increase the oven temperature to 400°F. Bake for 15 more minutes, until the top turns golden brown and a toothpick inserted in the center comes out clean or the internal temperature reaches between 190°F and 200°F. Allow the bread to slightly cool in the loaf pan, about 10 minutes, before transferring to a wire rack to cool completely, at least 2 hours.

Storage: Wrap the loaf or individual slices in plastic wrap, and store at room temperature for up to 5 days.

Ingredient tip: You can use applesauce instead of pear purée, especially if you don't have a food processor. Purchase store-bought gluten-free oat flour, or make it yourself by processing gluten-free oats in a high-speed blender or food processor.

Orange-Cranberry Bread

OIL-FREE • PREP AHEAD • SOY-FREE | Makes: 1 loaf (10 to 12 slices)

Prep time: 30 minutes, plus 20 minutes to rest
Bake time: 1 hour 10 minutes | **Cooling time:** 2 hours
Equipment: Box grater, hand mixer or stand mixer,
8½-by-4½-inch or 9-by-5-inch loaf pan

When I asked friends and family what baking flavors they loved, a few people responded with an orange-cranberry combination. At first bite, this bread surpassed my expectations! Now when I think about eating a slice, I envision a comforting fall morning, cup of tea in hand and snuggled under a warm blanket.

½ cup coconut sugar, monk fruit sweetener, or granulated sugar

Grated zest and juice of 1 orange (about 3 tablespoons each zest and juice)

¾ cup full-fat coconut milk or unsweetened almond milk

1 cup almond flour

¾ cup brown rice flour

¼ cup tapioca flour

1 teaspoon baking powder

½ teaspoon baking soda

¼ teaspoon sea salt

2 tablespoons maple syrup

½ teaspoon orange extract (optional)

½ teaspoon vanilla extract

½ to 1 cup halved fresh cranberries (you can use frozen, but thaw and halve first)

1. In a large bowl or stand mixer, combine the coconut sugar and orange zest. Use your fingers to rub together until fragrant, 20 to 30 seconds.

2. In a small bowl, combine the orange juice with the coconut milk. Whisk and set aside.

3. To the bowl with the sugar and orange zest, add the almond flour, brown rice flour, tapioca flour, baking powder, baking soda, and salt. Stir until blended.

4. To the bowl with the orange juice and milk, add the maple syrup, orange extract (if using), and vanilla. Whisk until combined.

5. Pour the wet ingredients into the flour mixture, and beat until a batter forms. Fold in the cranberries. Allow the batter to rest in the bowl at room temperature for 20 minutes.

6. Meanwhile, preheat the oven to 350°F. Line a 8½-by-4½-inch or 9-by-5-inch loaf pan with parchment paper.

7. Using a spatula, mix the batter a few times before transferring it to the prepared loaf pan. Bake for 1 hour to 1 hour 10 minutes, until the top turns golden brown and a toothpick inserted in the center comes out clean. To prevent the top of the bread from browning too much, lay a piece of aluminum foil over the pan for the last 10 minutes of cook time. Allow the bread to completely cool in the pan for at least 2 hours.

Storage: Wrap the loaf or individual slices in plastic wrap, and store at room temperature for up to 4 days.

Ingredient tip: This recipe calls for halved cranberries to ensure whole cranberries do not weigh the batter down, which would prevent rising and cause sinking in the middle as the bread cools.

Prep tip: Remember to zest the orange before juicing it. To easily squeeze the juice from the orange, roll it a few times on a hard surface applying pressure, then cut it in half. Use a fork to loosen the flesh before squeezing.

Chocolate Chip Zucchini Bread

OIL-FREE • PREP AHEAD • SOY-FREE | **Makes:** 1 loaf (10 to 12 slices)

Prep time: 30 minutes, plus 20 minutes to rest
Cook time: 1 hour | **Cooling time:** 2 hours
Equipment: Box grater, hand mixer or stand mixer, high-speed blender,
8½-by-4½-inch or 9-by-5-inch loaf pan

This bread recipe epitomizes balance: vegetables and chocolate! What a wonderful way to sneak in some greens, whether for yourself or your loved ones. Enjoy a slice as a sweet treat or a nutritious snack. This bread offers the best of both worlds. I suggest using the Enjoy Life brand of dairy-free chocolate chips in this bread.

½ cup full-fat coconut milk or unsweetened almond milk

½ teaspoon apple cider vinegar

1 cup almond flour

¾ cup brown rice flour

⅓ cup coconut sugar or monk fruit sweetener

2 tablespoons tapioca flour

2 teaspoons ground cinnamon

1 teaspoon baking powder

½ teaspoon baking soda

¼ teaspoon sea salt

¼ cup creamy almond butter

2 tablespoons unsweetened applesauce

2 tablespoons maple syrup

1 teaspoon vanilla extract

1 cup grated zucchini, squeezed dry and packed (about 1 medium zucchini)

¼ cup dairy-free chocolate chips

1. In a medium bowl, combine the coconut milk with the vinegar. Whisk and set aside.

2. In a large bowl or stand mixer, combine the almond flour, brown rice flour, coconut sugar, tapioca flour, cinnamon, baking powder, baking soda, and salt. Stir until blended.

3. To the bowl with the coconut milk and vinegar, add the almond butter, applesauce, maple syrup, and vanilla. Whisk until creamy, or transfer to a high-speed blender and mix well.

4. Pour the wet ingredients into the flour mixture and beat until a batter forms. Fold in the grated zucchini and chocolate chips. Allow the batter to rest in the bowl at room temperature for 20 minutes.

5. Preheat the oven to 350°F. Line a 8½-by-4½-inch or 9-by-5-inch loaf pan with parchment paper.

6. Using a spatula, mix the batter a few times before transferring it to the prepared loaf pan. Bake for 55 minutes to 1 hour, until a toothpick inserted in the center comes out clean. Allow the bread to completely cool in the loaf pan for at least 2 hours.

Storage: Wrap the loaf or individual slices in plastic wrap, and store at room temperature for up to 4 days.

Prep tip: I use a terry cloth washcloth to wring zucchini dry because it is much more absorbent than paper towels. If you have the time and want to ensure the grated zucchini is completely dry, allow it to sit in a strainer for 1 hour before baking, then wring out any excess water with a towel. Wet zucchini will weigh down the batter, alter the texture, and affect the baking time.

Cinnamon Raisin Bread

OIL-FREE • PREP AHEAD • SOY-FREE | **Makes:** 1 loaf (10 slices)

Prep time: 20 minutes, plus 15 minutes to rest
Cook time: 1 hour 5 minutes | **Cooling time:** 2 hours 10 minutes
Equipment: 8½-by-4½-inch or 9-by-5-inch loaf pan, hand
mixer or stand mixer, food thermometer (optional)

Growing up, I had my pick of two types of toast in the morning: plain or cinnamon raisin. Can you guess which one I chose the majority of the time? I will admit that back then, it was not homemade, which is what makes this bread so special to me. There is something about baking a food that makes you think fondly of the past while also knowing you had a hand in making it a bit more authentic. With the sweetness found in the cinnamon swirl center, there is no wonder I choose it to this day!

FOR THE BREAD

2 flax eggs (2 tablespoons
    ground flaxseed and
    4 tablespoons water)
¾ cup full-fat coconut milk
1 teaspoon apple cider vinegar
1¼ cups brown rice flour
½ cup almond flour
⅓ cup coconut sugar
2 tablespoons gluten-
    free oat flour
2 tablespoons tapioca flour
2 teaspoons ground cinnamon
1½ teaspoons baking powder
½ teaspoon baking soda
¼ teaspoon sea salt
¼ cup unsweetened
    applesauce
2 tablespoons maple syrup
1 teaspoon vanilla extract
½ cup raisins

1. Preheat the oven to 350°F. Line a 8½-by-4½-inch or 9-by-5-inch loaf pan with parchment paper.

2. In a small bowl, prepare the flax eggs by whisking together the ground flaxseed and water. Set aside for at least 10 minutes.

3. In a medium bowl, combine the coconut milk and vinegar. Whisk and set aside.

4. In a large bowl or stand mixer, combine the brown rice flour, almond flour, coconut sugar, oat flour, tapioca flour, cinnamon, baking powder, baking soda, and salt. Stir to blend.

5. To the bowl with the coconut milk and vinegar, add the flax eggs, applesauce, maple syrup, and vanilla. Whisk until creamy.

6. Pour the wet ingredients into the flour mixture. Beat until a batter forms. Fold in the raisins. Let the batter rest in the bowl at room temperature for 15 minutes.

½ cup coconut sugar

**1 tablespoon ground
    cinnamon**

7. To make the cinnamon swirl, in a small bowl, mix the coconut sugar and cinnamon.

8. Transfer a third of the batter into the bottom of the prepared loaf pan. Sprinkle with half of the cinnamon swirl. Add another third of the batter on top, and sprinkle with the remaining cinnamon swirl. Add the remaining batter, using a wetted spatula to make sure it is evenly distributed in the pan.

9. Bake for 50 minutes. Cover with aluminum foil and increase the oven temperature to 375°F. Bake for 15 more minutes, or until the internal temperature reaches between 190°F and 200°F. Allow the bread to cool for 5 to 10 minutes in the loaf pan, then transfer to a wire rack to cool completely, about 2 hours.

Storage: Wrap the loaf or individual slices in plastic wrap, and store at room temperature for up to 4 days.

Sweet Potato Rolls

PREP AHEAD • SOY-FREE | **Makes:** 10 to 12 rolls

Prep time: 30 minutes, plus 2 hours to rise
Cook time: 35 minutes | **Cooling time:** 15 minutes
Equipment: Food thermometer (optional), hand mixer or stand mixer,
food processor (optional), 9-by-13-inch baking dish, food thermometer (optional)

Sweet potato rolls used to be one of my favorite big-gathering appetizers,
but ever since going gluten-free, I have had to (unfortunately) pass on
them. Knowing that there is an option I can make at home makes me
feel so much better about it. I typically use Japanese sweet potato in
this recipe because I love the unique sweetness the variety provides, but
you can use regular as well. Enjoy with some vegan butter or blackberry-
chia jam (see Blackberry-Chia Jam Thumbprint Cookies, page 78).

1 cup unsweetened
   almond milk

3 tablespoons maple syrup

1 (¼-ounce) packet
   dry active yeast

3 cups gluten-free all-
   purpose flour

1 teaspoon sea salt

1 medium Japanese or
   regular sweet potato,
   baked and mashed

¼ cup extra-virgin olive oil

Nonstick cooking spray

1. In a small saucepan, heat the almond milk over medium heat for 3 to 5 minutes, until warm to the touch but not too hot. If using a food thermometer, it should be about 115°F. Remove from the heat and add the maple syrup. Transfer to a small bowl or 1-quart measuring cup, and stir in the yeast. Set aside for 10 minutes.

2. In a large bowl or stand mixer, combine the flour and salt. Stir to blend.

3. In a food processor, combine the mashed sweet potato and olive oil, and blend until creamy, 10 to 20 seconds. If you don't have a food processor, whisk the ingredients together vigorously with a fork. Transfer to the bowl with the flour mixture.

4. Start beating the sweet potato mixture at a low speed, and slowly incorporate the proofed yeast. Increase the speed to medium and beat until a thick dough forms. Use a spatula to fold the dough a few times to make sure everything blends together.

5. Spray a medium bowl with cooking spray, and place the dough inside the bowl. Lightly cover the bowl with plastic wrap, and allow to rise at room temperature for 1 hour.

6. Spray a 9-by-13-inch baking dish with cooking spray or line the bottom with parchment paper. With well-floured hands, gather ⅓ to ½ cup of the dough and gently roll it into a ball. Repeat with the remaining dough. Place the balls of dough side by side (they can be touching) in the prepared baking dish. Lightly cover with plastic wrap, and allow the rolls to rise for 1 more hour.

7. Meanwhile, preheat the oven to 375°F.

8. Bake for 30 to 35 minutes, until the outside turns slightly golden brown and firm to the touch or the internal temperature reaches 190°F (bake time will depend on the size of your rolls). Allow the rolls to cool in the baking dish for 10 to 15 minutes. Serve warm.

Storage: I recommend enjoying these rolls immediately. Otherwise, lightly cover them in aluminum foil, and store at room temperature for up to 2 days.

Prep tip: This dough is sticky, so when forming rolls, wash your hands after every fourth roll or so, then re-flour your hands.

"Cheesy" Crackers

GRAIN-FREE • PREP AHEAD • SOY-FREE | **Makes:** about 40 crackers

---

Prep time: 10 minutes, plus 30 minutes to chill
Cook time: 15 minutes | **Cooling time:** 5 minutes
Equipment: Hand mixer or stand mixer, two baking sheets, rolling pin

When I couldn't find a gluten-free cracker that I loved on store shelves, I started to make my own. Nutritional yeast (an inactive form of yeast grown and harvested from molasses) has a savory, nutty taste and tends to be a great vegan cheese substitute.

2 flax eggs (2 tablespoons ground flaxseed and 4 tablespoons water)

1¾ cups almond flour

¼ cup nutritional yeast

½ teaspoon sea salt

¼ cup melted coconut oil

Nonstick cooking spray (for greasing)

1. In a small bowl, prepare the flax eggs by whisking together the ground flaxseed and water. Set aside for at least 10 minutes.

2. In a large bowl or stand mixer, combine the almond flour, nutritional yeast, and salt. Stir to blend.

3. Add the flax eggs to the flour mixture. Start to beat on low speed, slowly incorporating the melted coconut oil until a crumbly dough forms. Gather the dough into a ball, wrap it tightly in plastic wrap, and refrigerate for 30 minutes.

4. Preheat the oven to 350°F. Line two baking sheets with parchment paper.

5. Place the ball of dough between two sheets of parchment paper. Using a rolling pin, roll the ball of dough between the parchment paper until about ¼ inch thick. Using a greased pizza cutter, cut into 1½- to 2-inch squares. Use a greased spatula to carefully place each cracker on the prepared baking sheets (they can be close together but not touching). Bake for 15 minutes, turning the pans halfway through to ensure even cooking.

6. Allow the crackers to slightly cool on the baking sheets, about 5 minutes, then transfer them to a wire rack.

Storage: Place the crackers in an airtight container or zip-top bag, and store in the pantry for up to 1 month.

"Butter" Crackers

GRAIN-FREE • SOY-FREE | **Makes:** 35 to 40 crackers

Prep time: 10 minutes | **Cook time:** 15 minutes | **Cooling time:** 5 minutes
Equipment: Baking sheet, hand mixer or stand mixer, rolling pin

Given their neutral (yet delicious) flavor, these crackers go well with just about anything. Since they keep so well, I pretty much always have them on hand. I love spreading them with hummus, guacamole, or dairy-free pesto and layering on olives, or raw or roasted vegetables. I've even used them for peanut butter crackers, which kids love just as much.

2 flax eggs (2 tablespoons ground flaxseed and 4 tablespoons water)

1½ cups almond flour

3 tablespoons tapioca flour

½ teaspoon sea salt

¼ cup melted vegan butter

Nonstick cooking spray (for greasing)

1. Preheat the oven to 350°F. Line a baking sheet with parchment paper.

2. In a small bowl, prepare the flax eggs by whisking together the ground flaxseed and water. Set aside for at least 10 minutes.

3. In a large bowl or stand mixer, combine the almond flour, tapioca flour, and salt. Stir to blend.

4. Add the flax eggs to the flour mixture. Start to beat on low speed, slowly incorporating the melted vegan butter until a crumbly dough forms. Using your hands, gather the dough into a ball.

5. Place the ball of dough between two sheets of parchment paper. Using a rolling pin, roll the ball of dough between the parchment paper sheets until about an ⅛ to ¼ inch thick. Using a greased pizza cutter to cut into 1½- to 2-inch squares. Use a greased spatula to carefully place each cracker on the prepared baking sheet (they can be close together but not touching). Bake for 15 minutes, turning the pan halfway through to ensure even cooking.

6. Allow the crackers to slightly cool on the baking sheet, about 5 minutes, then transfer them to a wire rack.

Storage: Place the crackers in an airtight container or zip-top bag, and store in the pantry for up to 1 month.

Chocolate Cookies with Buttercream Filling, page 86

COOKIES, BROWNIES, AND BARS

Fudgy Brownies

PREP AHEAD • SOY-FREE | Serves: 9

Prep time: 20 minutes | **Cook time:** 30 minutes | **Cooling time:** 2 hours
Equipment: 8-by-8-inch baking dish, hand mixer or stand mixer

It has been a secret dream of mine to create the ultimate brownie. This is no small feat! These are not your traditional cake-like brownies. *Fudgy* and *dense* are the words I would use to describe them. I have shared them with some self-proclaimed chocoholics and children (my true critics) and have received positive feedback from both. The pumpkin purée gives the brownies a moist texture and boosts the nutritional benefits. This is a fudgy brownie you can feel good about.

Nonstick cooking spray

2 flax eggs (2 tablespoons ground flaxseed and 4 tablespoons water)

½ cup dairy-free chocolate chips

2 tablespoons coconut oil

¾ cup coconut sugar

¾ cup brown rice flour

½ cup unsweetened cocoa powder

¼ cup almond flour

¼ cup tapioca flour

½ teaspoon baking powder

¼ teaspoon sea salt

¾ cup full-fat coconut milk or unsweetened almond milk

⅓ cup pumpkin purée

⅓ cup maple syrup

1 teaspoon vanilla extract

1. Preheat the oven to 350°F. Spray an 8-by-8-inch baking dish with cooking spray, or line it with parchment paper.

2. In a medium bowl, prepare the flax eggs by whisking together the ground flaxseed and water. Set aside for at least 10 minutes.

3. In a small saucepan over medium heat, combine the chocolate chips and coconut oil. Heat until melted, 2 to 3 minutes, stirring frequently (be careful not to let it burn). Remove the saucepan from the heat and set aside.

4. In a large bowl or stand mixer, mix the coconut sugar, brown rice flour, cocoa powder, almond flour, tapioca flour, baking powder, and salt. Stir until blended.

5. To the bowl with the flax eggs, add the coconut milk, pumpkin purée, maple syrup, and vanilla. Whisk until creamy.

6. Pour the wet ingredients into the flour mixture, and start beating on medium speed. Slowly incorporate the melted chocolate mixture, and continue to beat, increasing the speed as needed, until a batter forms. Transfer the batter to the prepared baking dish.

7. Bake for 27 to 30 minutes, until the edges have started to crust and pull away from the sides of the baking dish. (The middle will still "jiggle" and appear darker and undercooked, but it will set as it cools.) Allow the brownies to cool completely in the baking dish, about 2 hours, before cutting into 9 brownies.

Storage: Wrap individual brownies in plastic wrap, and store at room temperature for up to 3 days or in the refrigerator for up to 5 days.

Chocolate Chip Cookies

PREP AHEAD • SOY-FREE | **Makes:** 14 to 16 cookies

Prep time: 10 minutes, plus 30 minutes to chill
Cook time: 15 minutes | **Cooling time:** 20 minutes
Equipment: Hand mixer or stand mixer, two baking sheets

Not only does everyone deserve to enjoy chocolate chip cookies, but everyone also deserves to make a memory baking them. I remember being about five years old, wearing an adult-sized apron, helping my mom at the counter while we created this classical confection—I believe my love for baking dates all the way back to that moment! I love using cashew butter in this recipe because its creamy sweetness aligns well with cookie dough. And without the raw eggs, there's no reason not to sneak a taste before slipping them in the oven.

1 flax egg (1 tablespoon ground flaxseed and 2 tablespoons water)

1 cup almond flour

½ cup coconut sugar

¼ cup brown rice flour

½ teaspoon baking soda

¼ teaspoon sea salt

¼ cup plus 2 tablespoons melted coconut oil or melted vegan butter

⅓ cup creamy nut butter or seed butter (I suggest cashew or almond butter)

1 teaspoon vanilla extract

½ cup dairy-free chocolate chips

1. In a medium bowl, prepare the flax egg by whisking together the ground flaxseed and water. Set aside for at least 10 minutes.

2. In a large bowl or stand mixer, combine the almond flour, coconut sugar, brown rice flour, baking soda, and salt. Stir to blend.

3. To the bowl with the flax egg, add the melted coconut oil, nut butter, and vanilla. Whisk until creamy.

4. Pour the wet ingredients into the flour mixture, and beat until a dough forms. Gently fold in the chocolate chips. Gather the dough in a ball. Wrap tightly in plastic wrap and refrigerate for 30 minutes.

5. Meanwhile, preheat the oven to 350°F. Line two baking sheets with parchment paper.

6. Once the dough has chilled, gather about 2 tablespoons of dough at a time and place on the prepared baking sheets at least 2 inches apart. Bake for 12 to 15 minutes (less time for a chewier cookie). The cookies will look undercooked when you take them out, but they will firm up as they cool. Allow the cookies to cool on the baking sheets for at least 15 to 20 minutes before serving.

Storage: Cover loosely with aluminum foil, and store at room temperature for up to 4 days. You can also store them loosely covered in the refrigerator, but the cold temperature will cause them to get crispier.

Easy Almond Butter Chocolate Bars

GRAIN-FREE • PREP AHEAD • SOY-FREE | Serves: 9

Prep time: 20 minutes | **Bake time:** 50 minutes | **Cooling time:** 4 hours
Equipment: 8-by-8-inch baking dish, hand mixer or stand mixer, food processor

This dish is an easy answer to almost any situation that calls for something sweet. Whether your child wants to get creative in the kitchen or you're hosting a small get-together for your friends, these brownie-like bars go over well with almost anyone.

FOR THE CRUST

1¼ cups almond flour

3 tablespoons coconut sugar

2 tablespoons arrowroot starch or tapioca flour

1 tablespoon unsweetened cocoa powder (optional)

¼ teaspoon sea salt

⅓ cup melted coconut oil

1 teaspoon vanilla extract

FOR THE FILLING

1¾ cups creamy almond butter

½ cup pumpkin purée

⅓ cup maple syrup or coconut nectar

¼ cup coconut sugar

2 tablespoons arrowroot starch

1 tablespoon full-fat coconut milk

1 teaspoon vanilla extract

¼ teaspoon sea salt

½ cup dairy-free chocolate chips

1. Preheat the oven to 350°F. Line an 8-by-8-inch baking dish with parchment paper.

2. To make the crust, in a large bowl or stand mixer, mix the almond flour, coconut sugar, arrowroot starch, cocoa powder, and salt. Stir to blend.

3. In a small bowl, whisk together the melted coconut oil and vanilla. Pour the wet ingredients into the flour mixture, and beat until a crumbly dough forms (it should feel like damp sand). Press the dough into the bottom of the pre-pared baking dish. Bake for 15 minutes, and set aside.

4. Meanwhile, make the filling. In a food processor, combine the almond butter, pumpkin purée, maple syrup, coconut sugar, arrowroot starch, coconut milk, vanilla, and salt. Blend until creamy. Add the chocolate chips, and blend again until they are fully incorporated into the almond butter mixture.

5. Using a spatula or large spoon, transfer the filling to the baking dish with the crust. Bake for 30 to 35 minutes, until the edges are golden brown and have started to pull away from the baking dish. Allow the bars to completely cool in the baking dish, about 2 hours, then transfer them to the refrigerator for at least 2 hours to completely set before cutting into nine bars.

Storage: Place the bars in an airtight container in the refrigerator for up to 5 days; or wrap individual bars in plastic wrap, and store in the refrigerator for up to 1 week.

Almond-Ginger Cookies

GRAIN-FREE • PREP AHEAD • SOY-FREE | **Makes:** 13 to 15 cookies

Prep time: 20 minutes | **Cook time:** 15 minutes | **Cooling time:** 1 hour 10 minutes
Equipment: Box grater, two baking sheets, hand mixer or stand mixer

These almond-ginger cookies were some of the first grain-free cookies I ever made, and while I have always had an affinity for cookies of the chocolate variety, I loved the flavor immediately. Adding the pumpkin pie spice lends to their uniqueness, but it's not necessary. I also love the molasses in these cookies as it is a sweetener that pairs perfectly with their flavor.

1 flax egg (1 tablespoon ground flaxseed and 2 tablespoons water)

1½ cups almond flour

½ cup coconut sugar

¼ cup coconut flour

1 tablespoon grated peeled ginger

2 teaspoons ground cinnamon

2 teaspoons baking soda

1 teaspoon pumpkin pie spice (or ½ teaspoon ground cloves and ½ teaspoon ground nutmeg) (optional)

¼ teaspoon sea salt

⅓ cup melted vegan butter

¼ cup blackstrap molasses

1 teaspoon vanilla extract

1. Preheat the oven to 350°F. Line two baking sheets with parchment paper.

2. In a medium bowl, prepare the flax egg by whisking together the ground flaxseed and water. Set aside for at least 10 minutes.

3. In a large bowl or stand mixer, combine the almond flour, coconut sugar, coconut flour, ginger, cinnamon, baking soda, pumpkin pie spice (if using), and salt. Stir to blend.

4. To the bowl with the flax egg, add the melted vegan butter, molasses, and vanilla. Whisk until creamy.

5. Pour the wet ingredients into the flour mixture, and beat until a batter forms.

6. Spoon 2 tablespoons of dough at a time, placing them 2 to 3 inches apart on the prepared baking sheets. Bake for 12 to 15 minutes, until the edges are firm to the touch but the center is somewhat soft (for a chewier cookie, bake for less time). Allow the cookies to cool slightly on the baking sheets, about 10 minutes, before transferring them to a wire rack to completely cool for about 1 hour.

Storage: Cover loosely with aluminum foil, and store at room temperature for up to 4 days.

Sugar Cookies with Vanilla Icing

GRAIN-FREE • PREP AHEAD • SOY-FREE | **Makes:** 16 cookies

Prep time: 20 minutes, plus 30 minutes to chill
Cook time: 15 minutes | **Cooling time:** 30 minutes
Equipment: Hand mixer or stand mixer, two baking sheets, rolling pin, cookie cutter

Of course, these sugar cookies are delicious enough on their own (they are sugar cookies, after all), but the icing makes them that much better. The texture is slightly soft and chewy, yet they are stable enough to be decorated. Use this recipe any time of the year, knowing that the only thing that needs to change is your cookie cutter's shape.

FOR THE COOKIES

1¼ cups almond flour

¼ cup coconut flour

¼ cup arrowroot starch

½ teaspoon baking soda

¼ teaspoon sea salt

½ cup vegan butter

½ cup monk fruit sweetener
   or granulated sugar

1 tablespoon full-fat
   coconut milk

1 teaspoon vanilla extract

Nonstick cooking spray

FOR THE VANILLA ICING

1 cup coconut butter

3 tablespoons coconut
   oil, softened

1 teaspoon vanilla extract

1. In a large bowl or stand mixer, mix the almond flour, coconut flour, arrowroot starch, baking soda, and salt. Stir to blend.

2. In a separate large bowl, mix the vegan butter and monk fruit sweetener, and cream them together. Add the coconut milk and vanilla, and beat again.

3. Start beating the flour mixture on low to medium speed, slowly incorporating the butter mixture, about ¼ cup at a time, until a crumbly dough forms (the dough will appear dry at first, but that's okay). Use your hands to gather the dough in a ball, kneading everything together as you do. Wrap tightly in plastic wrap and refrigerate for 30 minutes.

4. Meanwhile, preheat the oven to 350°F. Line two baking sheets with parchment paper.

5. Place the dough between two sheets of parchment paper. Using a rolling pin, roll the dough out to ¼ to ½ inch thick (the thicker the cookie, the chewier it will be). Use a cookie cutter of desired shape and size, sprayed with cooking spray, to form cookies. Use a spatula sprayed with cooking spray to carefully place them on the prepared baking sheets. Continue to gather the dough, roll it out, and cut more cookies until all of the dough is used.

6. Bake for 10 to 12 minutes. Allow the cookies to cool on the baking sheets for 20 to 30 minutes before transferring them to a wire rack to cool completely.

7. To make the vanilla icing, in a small saucepan, combine the coconut butter and coconut oil over low heat. Cook until just melted, 3 to 5 minutes, stirring frequently with a fork and breaking up any clumps (be careful not to let the coconut butter burn). Remove the saucepan from the heat, and transfer the mixture to a small glass or ceramic bowl. Allow the mixture to cool for 10 minutes, then whisk in the vanilla. Spoon about 1 tablespoon icing over each cookie.

Storage: Cover loosely with aluminum foil, and store at room temperature for up to 1 week. The cookies will also keep in the refrigerator for up to 2 weeks but will harden when cold. I suggest bringing them to room temperature before serving.

Soft and Chewy Peanut Butter Cookies

GRAIN-FREE • OIL-FREE • PREP AHEAD • SOY-FREE | **Makes:** 12 cookies

Prep time: 15 minutes, plus 30 minutes to chill
Cook time: 15 minutes | **Cooling time:** 30 minutes
Equipment: Hand mixer or stand mixer, two baking sheets

Some cookies are better crispy, but these soft and chewy cookies capture peanut butter's essential taste and texture. They are indulgent enough to be dessert, yet I believe they make a great snack or even a quick breakfast option! Make them in advance to grab and go throughout your week.

1½ cups almond flour

¼ cup coconut flour

¼ cup coconut sugar

½ teaspoon baking powder

½ teaspoon baking soda

¼ teaspoon sea salt

⅓ cup full-fat coconut milk or unsweetened almond milk

1 ripe banana, mashed

¼ cup creamy peanut butter

2 tablespoons maple syrup or coconut nectar

1 teaspoon vanilla extract

Nonstick cooking spray (optional)

1. In a large bowl or stand mixer, mix the almond flour, coconut flour, coconut sugar, baking powder, baking soda, and salt. Stir to blend.

2. In a medium bowl, mix the coconut milk, mashed banana, peanut butter, maple syrup, and vanilla. Whisk until creamy.

3. Pour the wet ingredients into the flour mixture, and beat until a batter forms. Gather the dough into a ball (it will be sticky!). Wrap it tightly in plastic wrap and refrigerate for 30 minutes.

4. Meanwhile, preheat the oven to 350°F. Line two baking sheets with parchment paper.

5. Gather about 2 tablespoons of dough, and use your hands to roll it into a ball. Flatten to about ½ inch thick, and place on a the prepared baking sheets. Repeat with the remaining dough, spacing the cookies about 2 inches apart. If desired, use a fork sprayed with cooking spray to create a crisscross pattern on the tops.

6. Bake for 10 to 12 minutes, until the tops are golden brown and the cookies are slightly firm to the touch. Allow the cookies to slightly cool on the baking sheets, about 10 minutes, before transferring to a wire rack to cool for at least 20 more minutes before serving.

Storage: Cover loosely with aluminum foil or plastic wrap, and store in the refrigerator for up to 5 days.

Prep tip: If the dough gets sticky as you are forming your cookies, rinse your hands every third or fourth one.

Maple Pecan Bars

GRAIN-FREE OPTION • PREP AHEAD • SOY-FREE | Serves: 9

Prep time: 30 minutes | **Cook time:** 45 minutes | **Cooling time:** 6 hours
Equipment: 8-by-8-inch baking dish, hand mixer or stand mixer

Like a Southern-style blondie, these maple pecan bars are soft and gooey, yet their nutty crunch gives them quite a unique texture! They are sweet and sticky, and have a melt-in-your-mouth effect that could please any audience. These are a perfect and easy dessert to serve to others or keep for yourself.

FOR THE CRUST

1½ cups brown rice flour or almond flour

2 tablespoons arrowroot starch

2 tablespoons coconut sugar

1 teaspoon ground cinnamon

⅓ cup melted coconut oil

1 teaspoon vanilla extract

FOR THE FILLING

½ cup coconut sugar or granulated sugar

⅓ cup melted coconut oil

⅓ cup maple syrup

2 cups roughly chopped pecans

3 tablespoons full-fat coconut milk

1 teaspoon vanilla extract

2 tablespoons arrowroot starch

1. Preheat the oven to 350°F. Line an 8-by-8-inch baking dish with parchment paper.

2. To make the crust, in a large bowl or stand mixer, mix the brown rice flour, arrowroot starch, coconut sugar, and cinnamon. Stir to blend.

3. In a small bowl, whisk together the melted coconut oil and vanilla.

4. While beating on medium speed, slowly pour the wet ingredients into the flour mixture and continue to beat until a crumbly dough forms, increasing the speed as needed. Press the dough into the bottom of the prepared baking dish. Bake for 15 minutes, then set aside until ready to use.

5. To make the filling, in a small saucepan, combine the coconut sugar, melted coconut oil, and maple syrup. Heat over medium-low heat and bring to a simmer. Once it has started to bubble, continue to cook for 1 to 2 minutes, stirring frequently, watching it carefully to make sure it doesn't burn. Remove the saucepan from the heat, and allow the mixture to cool for about 10 minutes (the mixture may become discolored as it cools, but that is normal; just whisk it away).

6. Meanwhile, place the chopped pecans in another large bowl and set aside. Once the coconut oil mixture has cooled, add the coconut milk and vanilla to the saucepan and whisk. Pour the mixture over the chopped pecans in the large bowl, and stir until combined. Add the arrowroot starch, and stir again. Pour the mixture over the crust in the baking dish.

7. Bake for 27 to 30 minutes, until the filling mixture bubbles. Allow the bars to cool completely in the baking dish, about 2 hours, then transfer to the refrigerator to allow to set for 4 hours or, ideally, overnight, before cutting into nine bars.

Storage: Store the bars in the refrigerator, covered or uncovered, for up to 1 week. I recommend letting them sit out at room temperature for 20 minutes before serving.

Oatmeal-Raisin Cookies

PREP AHEAD • SOY-FREE | **Makes:** 16 cookies

Prep time: 15 minutes, plus 20 minutes to chill
Cook time: 15 minutes | **Cooling time:** 30 minutes
Equipment: Hand mixer or stand mixer, two baking sheets

I appreciate oatmeal raisin cookies so much more now that I'm an adult. Growing up, I couldn't understand why someone would want to eat a cookie without chocolate, but I get it now. These cookies have a delightfully chewy texture with a subtle sweetness that results in quite a delicious sweet treat. I often eat these for breakfast; they make a great option for dessert (since chocolate naturally has caffeine). I love them plain or with extra nut butter on top.

1 flax egg (1 tablespoon ground flaxseed and 2 tablespoons water)

1 cup almond flour or brown rice flour

1 cup gluten-free rolled oats

½ cup coconut sugar

1 teaspoon ground cinnamon

1 teaspoon baking powder

½ teaspoon baking soda

¼ teaspoon sea salt

⅓ cup creamy almond butter

¼ cup plus 2 tablespoons melted coconut oil

¼ cup maple syrup

1 teaspoon vanilla extract

½ cup raisins

1. In a medium bowl, prepare the flax egg by whisking together the ground flaxseed and water. Set aside for at least 10 minutes.

2. In a large bowl or stand mixer, mix the almond flour, oats, coconut sugar, cinnamon, baking powder, baking soda, and salt. Stir to blend.

3. To the bowl with the flax egg, add the almond butter, melted coconut oil, maple syrup, and vanilla. Whisk until creamy.

4. Pour the wet ingredients into the flour mixture. Beat until a crumbly dough forms. Add the raisins and beat again. The mixture may appear dry at first, but that's okay. Use your hands to gather the dough in a ball and knead everything together. Wrap tightly in plastic wrap and refrigerate for 20 minutes (once chilled, the coconut oil will help hold everything together).

5. Meanwhile, preheat the oven to 350°F. Line two baking sheets with parchment paper.

6. Gather about 2 tablespoons of dough, and use your hands to roll it into a ball. Place them about 2 inches apart on the prepared baking sheets.

7. Bake for 10 to 12 minutes, until golden brown. The cookies will be soft to the touch when you take them out of the oven, but they will firm as they cool. Allow the cookies to cool on the baking sheets, about 30 minutes, before serving.

Storage: Place the cookies side by side on a plate, or if you need to stack them, use a piece of parchment paper in between cookies to prevent sticking. Cover loosely with aluminum foil, and store at room temperature for up to 1 week.

Macadamia Nut Cookies

SOY-FREE | **Makes:** 12 to 14 cookies

Prep time: 10 minutes | **Cook time:** 15 minutes | **Cooling time:** 30 minutes
Equipment: Two baking sheets, hand mixer or stand mixer

The macadamia nuts are the star of the show in these cookies. Each bite provides that sweet, nutty, and creamy crunch. While you can use either raw or roasted nuts in this recipe, I highly recommend roasted because it enhances the nuts' flavor.

1 flax egg (1 tablespoon ground flaxseed and 2 tablespoons water)

1 cup almond flour

⅓ cup brown rice flour

½ teaspoon baking soda

¼ teaspoon sea salt

½ cup vegan butter, cut into 1-inch pieces

½ cup coconut sugar

2 teaspoons vanilla extract

2 tablespoons maple syrup

½ cup roughly chopped macadamia nuts (raw or roasted)

1. Preheat the oven to 350°F. Line two baking sheets with parchment paper.

2. In a small bowl, prepare the flax egg by whisking together the ground flaxseed and water. Set aside for at least 10 minutes.

3. In a large bowl or stand mixer, mix the almond flour, brown rice flour, baking soda, and salt. Stir to blend.

4. In a separate large bowl, mix the vegan butter and coconut sugar. Use your hands to massage the butter and sugar together. Then use a hand mixer to further cream them together until fluffy, 10 to 15 seconds. Mix the butter-sugar mixture with a spatula until fully combined.

5. In the bowl with the flax egg, whisk in the vanilla. Transfer the butter-sugar mixture to the flour mixture, and start beating on low. Increase the speed, and add the flax egg mixture. Add the maple syrup, and beat until a dough forms. Fold in the chopped macadamia nuts.

6. Gather about 2 tablespoons of dough at a time, and place on the prepared baking sheets (as is, no need to roll the dough into balls), spacing them about 3 inches apart.

7. Bake for 10 to 12 minutes, until the edges have started to firm up. The center of the cookies will look undercooked, but they will firm up as they cool. Allow the cookies to cool for about 30 minutes on the baking sheets before serving.

Storage: Cover loosely with aluminum foil, and store in the refrigerator for up to 1 week.

Ingredient tip: If you want to use roasted macadamia nuts (roasting enhances their flavor), buy them roasted, or roast them on a baking sheet in a 400°F oven for 10 to 12 minutes.

Blackberry-Chia Jam Thumbprint Cookies

GRAIN-FREE OPTION • PREP AHEAD • SOY-FREE | **Makes:** 14 to 16 cookies

Prep time: 30 minutes, plus 30 minutes to chill
Bake time: 15 minutes | **Cooling time:** 30 minutes
Equipment: Hand mixer or stand mixer, two baking sheets

These cookies are like eating a nut butter and jelly sandwich, but better! They are the right amount of sweetness, complemented by the subtly tart taste of the blackberry-chia jam. They offer a fruity dessert option for your kids or yourself.

FOR THE BLACKBERRY-CHIA JAM

2 cups frozen blackberries

Juice of ½ lemon

¼ cup maple syrup

2 tablespoons chia seeds

FOR THE COOKIES

1 flax egg (1 tablespoon ground flaxseed and 2 tablespoons water)

1¾ cups almond flour or all-purpose gluten-free flour

⅓ cup coconut sugar

¼ cup coconut flour

½ teaspoon baking soda

¼ teaspoon sea salt

¼ cup plus 2 tablespoons melted coconut oil

⅓ cup creamy almond butter

¼ cup maple syrup

1 teaspoon vanilla extract

1. To make the blackberry-chia jam, in a medium saucepan over medium-high heat, mix the blackberries, lemon juice, and maple syrup. Cover and bring to a boil, about 5 minutes. Remove the lid and stir, breaking up the berries with the back of a wooden spoon. Reduce the heat to medium low and simmer until the liquid has reduced by half, 10 to 15 minutes.

2. Transfer the mixture to a small bowl, and add the chia seeds. For the first 5 to 10 minutes, stir frequently to prevent the chia seeds from clumping. Set aside to allow the mixture to gel and cool, 20 to 30 minutes.

3. To make the cookies, in a medium bowl, prepare the flax egg by whisking together the ground flaxseed and water. Set aside for at least 10 minutes.

4. In a large bowl or stand mixer, mix the almond flour, coconut sugar, coconut flour, baking soda, and salt. Stir to blend.

5. In the bowl with the flax egg, add the melted coconut oil, almond butter, maple syrup, and vanilla. Whisk until creamy.

6. Pour the wet ingredients into the flour mixture. Beat until a crumbly dough forms. Use your hands to gather the dough in a ball. Wrap it tightly in plastic wrap and refrigerate for 30 minutes.

7. Meanwhile, preheat the oven to 350°F. Line two baking sheets with parchment paper.

8. Gather 1½ to 2 tablespoons of dough at a time and roll into balls, placing them on the prepared baking sheets 2 to 3 inches apart. Use your thumb to press a shallow well in the center
of each. Fill the centers with a teaspoon of the blackberry-chia jam.

9. Bake for 12 to 15 minutes, until the edges are golden brown. The cookies will still feel slightly soft to the touch, but they will firm as they cool. Allow the cookies to cool at least 30 minutes on the baking sheets.

Storage: Cover loosely with aluminum foil, and store at room temperature for up to 3 days; or store uncovered in the refrigerator for up to 5 days.

Plan-ahead tip: The blackberry-chia jam can be made up to 4 days in advance. Store in an airtight container in the refrigerator.

Grain-Free Gingerbread Men

GRAIN-FREE • PREP AHEAD • SOY-FREE | **Makes:** 12 cookies

Prep time: 15 minutes, plus 1 hour to chill
Cook time: 15 minutes | **Cooling time:** 1 hour 20 minutes
Equipment: Box grater, hand mixer or stand mixer, two
baking sheets, rolling pin, cookie cutter

This is my go-to holiday gingerbread man recipe. They are so easy to make and even more fun to frost. Bake them as an activity for the kids and kids at heart alike (I can personally attest to that!). No one would believe they are grain-free and vegan.

FOR THE COOKIES

1½ cups almond flour

¼ cup coconut flour

2 teaspoons grated peeled ginger

1 teaspoon ground cinnamon

½ teaspoon ground cloves

¼ teaspoon baking soda

¼ teaspoon sea salt

¼ cup blackstrap molasses

¼ cup melted coconut oil

3 tablespoons maple syrup, divided

Nonstick cooking spray

FOR THE FROSTING (OPTIONAL)

¼ cup coconut butter, softened

¼ cup vegan butter

¼ teaspoon vanilla extract

1. In a large bowl or stand mixer, mix the almond flour, coconut flour, ginger, cinnamon, cloves, baking soda, and salt. Stir to blend.

2. In a medium bowl, mix the molasses, melted coconut oil, and 2 tablespoons of maple syrup. Whisk until creamy.

3. Pour the wet ingredients into the flour mixture, and beat until a crumbly dough forms. Add the remaining 1 tablespoon of maple syrup, and beat again. Gather the dough into a ball, kneading everything together if you need to, then wrap tightly in plastic wrap and refrigerate for 45 minutes to 1 hour.

4. Meanwhile, preheat the oven to 350°F. Line two baking sheets with parchment paper.

5. Place the ball of dough between two sheets of parchment paper. Using a rolling pin, roll the dough to about ¼ inch thick (a little thinner if you want a crispier cookie). Using a gingerbread man cookie cutter sprayed with cooking spray, cut the cookies. Peel away the extra dough, and using a spatula sprayed with cooking spray, carefully place the cookies on the prepared baking sheets. Continue to gather the dough, roll it out, and cut more cookies until all of the dough is used.

6. Bake for 10 to 12 minutes, until the edges have started to firm and turn a slight golden brown. The cookies should be slightly soft to the touch, but they will continue to firm as they cool. Allow the cookies to cool for about 20 minutes on the baking sheets before transferring them to a wire rack to cool completely, about 1 hour.

7. To make the frosting (if using), in a small bowl, combine the coconut butter, vegan butter, and vanilla. Stir until blended and creamy. Transfer the frosting to a plastic bag. Use scissors to cut a small tip off of one corner. Squeeze to pipe.

Storage: Cover loosely with aluminum foil, and store at room temperature for up to 5 days or in the refrigerator for up to 1 week. The cookies and frosting will harden a bit when cold.

Ingredient tip: For the frosting, I keep my coconut butter in a warm place so it stays soft. Otherwise, you can place the coconut butter in a glass Pyrex bowl directly on your stove top over low heat. Watch carefully (occasionally stirring with a fork) until the coconut butter is a creamy consistency (still somewhat solid, not melted).

Date Caramel Blondie Bars

GRAIN-FREE • PREP AHEAD • SOY-FREE | Serves: 9

Prep time: 30 minutes, plus 20 minutes to soak
Cook time: 30 minutes | **Cooling time:** 4 hours
Equipment: 8-by-8-inch baking dish, food processor

With these blondies, you will *feel* as if you're indulging in dessert, but these bars are actually packed with nutrition. Chickpeas are a good source of protein and fiber—as well as vitamin K, folate, and other vitamins and minerals. They are great in blondies, but rest assured, you can't taste them! You'll forget the chickpeas are even included because the peanut butter and date caramel combination is that good, making these bars as delicious as they are nutritious.

FOR THE DATE CARAMEL

2 cups (about 20) Medjool dates (with pits)
3 to 4 cups boiling water
1 teaspoon vanilla extract
Pinch sea salt

FOR THE BLONDIES

1 (15.5-ounce) can chickpeas, drained and rinsed
½ cup creamy peanut butter or creamy nut butter
3 tablespoons coconut sugar
3 tablespoons full-fat coconut milk or unsweetened almond milk
1 teaspoon baking powder
½ teaspoon baking soda
¼ teaspoon sea salt

1. To make the date caramel, preheat the oven to 350°F. Line an 8-by-8-inch baking dish with parchment paper.

2. In a medium bowl, soak the dates in the boiling water for 20 minutes.

3. Drain the dates, reserving 3 tablespoons of the soaking water. Peel the dates (the skin should easily come off) and remove the pits.

4. In a food processor, place the pitted dates, the reserved soaking water, vanilla, and salt. Blend for 20 to 30 seconds, scraping down the sides as needed, until creamy. Transfer the mixture to a small bowl and set aside.

5. To make the blondies, in the food processor, combine the chickpeas, peanut butter, coconut sugar, coconut milk, baking powder, baking soda, and salt. Process for about 30 seconds, scraping down the sides as needed, until everything combines and is creamy.

6. Reserving ¼ cup, add the date caramel to the food processor with the chickpea mixture. Blend again until everything combines and a sticky dough forms.

7. Using a wetted spatula, transfer the dough to the prepared baking dish until it is evenly spread.

8. Spoon the reserved date caramel onto the center of the dough (in a few dollops), and use the spatula (rewet if needed) to swirl until incorporated.

9. Bake for 28 to 30 minutes, until the edges are golden brown and have started to pull away from the sides of the baking dish. Allow the bars to completely cool in the baking dish, at least 2 hours, then transfer to the refrigerator for at least 2 more hours to completely set before cutting into nine bars.

Storage: These blondies are even better the next day! Place them in an airtight container, and store in the refrigerator for up to 5 days.

Plan-ahead tip: You can make the date caramel up to 4 days in advance. Store in an airtight container in the refrigerator.

Fig Square Cookies

GRAIN-FREE • PREP AHEAD • SOY-FREE | **Makes:** 20 cookies

Prep time: 30 minutes, plus 20 minutes to chill
Cook time: 20 minutes | **Cooling time:** 1 hour 10 minutes
Equipment: Two baking sheets, hand mixer or stand mixer, food processor, rolling pin

Nothing brought me so much joy as seeing my best friend's two-year-old enjoying one of these cookies. I created this cookie with him in mind, and for all the children with certain food sensitivities who might otherwise never know the taste of a traditional childhood treat. If you, your child, or another loved one can't have nuts, try substituting the almond flour with a different gluten-free flour of choice.

FOR THE FILLING

1 cup dried figs
Boiling water
1 teaspoon ground cinnamon
½ teaspoon vanilla extract
Pinch sea salt

FOR THE CRUST

1 flax egg (1 tablespoon ground flaxseed and 2 tablespoons water)
1 cup almond flour
¼ cup tapioca flour
2 tablespoons coconut flour
1 tablespoon coconut sugar
1 teaspoon ground cinnamon
½ teaspoon baking powder
½ teaspoon baking soda
¼ teaspoon sea salt
3 tablespoons unsweetened applesauce
3 tablespoons melted coconut oil
Nonstick cooking spray

1. Preheat the oven to 350°F. Line two baking sheets with parchment paper.

2. In a small bowl, place the dried figs, and cover them with boiling water. Soak for 10 minutes, until soft.

3. In a medium bowl, prepare the flax egg by whisking together the ground flaxseed and water. Set aside for at least 10 minutes.

4. In a large bowl or stand mixer, mix the almond flour, tapioca flour, coconut flour, coconut sugar, cinnamon, baking powder, baking soda, and salt. Stir to blend.

5. To the bowl with the flax egg, add the applesauce and melted coconut oil. Whisk until mixed.

6. Pour the wet ingredients into the flour mixture, and beat until a dough forms. Gather the dough into a ball, and wrap in plastic wrap. Refrigerate for 20 minutes.

7. Meanwhile, finish the filling. Drain the figs, roughly chop them, and transfer to a food processor. Add the cinnamon, vanilla, and salt. Blend until a sticky paste forms, 20 to 30 seconds, scraping down the sides as needed.

8. Divide the ball of dough in half and form two balls. Place one ball of dough between two sheets of parchment paper. Using a rolling pin, roll the dough into a ¼-inch-thick square. Peel away the top piece of parchment paper, and using a wetted spatula, spread the fig paste mixture on top in an even layer.

9. Place the second ball of dough between two sheets of parchment paper, and roll it out to roughly the same size as the first. Remove the top piece of parchment, carefully turn the dough onto the fig filling, and peel away the other piece of parchment paper.

10. Using a pizza cutter or knife sprayed with cooking spray, cut 1½- to 2-inch square cookies. Using a spatula sprayed with cooking spray, carefully place the cookies 1 to 2 inches apart on the prepared baking sheets. Bake for 10 minutes. Flip the cookies and bake another 5 to 7 minutes, until golden brown and slightly firm to the touch. Allow the cookies to cool slightly on the baking sheets, about 10 minutes, before transferring them to a wire rack to cool completely, at least 1 hour.

Storage: Place the cookies in an airtight container, and store in the refrigerator for up to 10 days.

Chocolate Cookies with Buttercream Filling

GRAIN-FREE • PREP AHEAD • SOY-FREE | **Makes:** 14 to 16 cookies

Prep time: 10 minutes, plus 1 hour 5 minutes to chill
Cook time: 15 minutes | **Cooling time:** 1 hour 40 minutes
Equipment: Hand mixer or stand mixer, baking sheet,
rolling pin, 2-inch cookie cutter (optional)

Did you love cookies and milk as a kid? Me too! When I think about cookies, so many memories from my childhood come rushing back. What I want is for adults and children alike to be able to create wonderful memories with both nutritious and delicious food. That is what these cookies represent. Enjoy on their own or with a glass of almond milk on the side.

FOR THE COOKIES

1½ cups almond flour

½ cup unsweetened cocoa powder

⅓ cup coconut sugar

¼ cup coconut flour

½ teaspoon baking soda

¼ teaspoon sea salt

4 tablespoons vegan butter

¼ cup full-fat coconut milk or unsweetened almond milk

1 tablespoon maple syrup

1 teaspoon vanilla extract

Nonstick cooking spray

1. In a large bowl or stand mixer, mix the almond flour, cocoa powder, coconut sugar, coconut flour, baking soda, and salt. Stir until blended, using your fingers or the back of a wooden spoon to break up any clumps as needed.

2. Add the vegan butter to the flour mixture. Use your hands to mix and massage the butter into the flour until a crumbly dough forms.

3. In a small bowl, whisk together the coconut milk, maple syrup, and vanilla.

4. Pour the wet ingredients into the flour mixture, and beat until a dough forms. Use your hands to gather the dough into a ball, wrap tightly in plastic wrap, and refrigerate for 1 hour.

5. Meanwhile, preheat the oven to 365°F. Line a baking sheet with parchment paper.

6. Place the ball of dough between two sheets of parchment paper. Using a rolling pin, roll out the ball of dough until ¼ inch thick. Use a 2-inch cookie cutter to form cookies. If you don't have one, you can use a sharp knife sprayed with cooking spray to form cookies, but this will affect the resulting shape. Use a spatula sprayed with cooking spray

¾ **cup coconut oil**

¾ **cup palm oil shortening**

⅓ **cup arrowroot starch
or tapioca flour**

⅛ **teaspoon sea salt**

¼ **cup plus 2 tablespoons
maple syrup**

2 **teaspoons vanilla extract**

to carefully place them on the prepared baking sheet at least 1 inch apart. Continue to gather the dough, roll it out, and cut more cookies until all of the dough is used. Transfer the baking sheet to the freezer for 5 minutes.

7. Bake for 10 to 12 minutes, or until the edges have started to crisp and the cookies are slightly firm to the touch. Allow the cookies to cool for 10 minutes on the baking sheet before transferring to a wire rack to cool completely, at least 1 hour.

8. To make the buttercream filling, in a large bowl, combine the coconut oil and palm oil shortening. Beat until fluffy, about 1 minute.

9. Add the arrowroot starch and salt, and beat again. Add the maple syrup and vanilla, and beat until everything combines, using a spatula to scrape down the sides as needed.

10. Mix the filling with a spatula. Use the filling immediately, or transfer to the refrigerator for 10 minutes for a more dense texture. Once the cookies have cooled completely, spoon a tablespoon of filling between two cookies. Gently press the top cookie down until the filling is evenly distributed between the two. Transfer the cookies to the refrigerator to set for at least 30 minutes.

Storage: Cover loosely with aluminum foil or place in an airtight container, and store in the refrigerator for up to 5 days.

Plan-ahead tip: You can make the buttercream filling up to 3 days in advance. Make sure you keep it in an airtight container at room temperature. Give it a good stir before using, as separation might occur.

Strawberry Cupcakes with Strawberry Frosting, page 92

CHAPTER FIVE

CAKES AND CUPCAKES

Chocolate Cupcakes with Peanut Butter Frosting

PREP AHEAD • SOY-FREE | **Makes:** 10 to 12 cupcakes

Prep time: 20 minutes | **Cook time:** 25 minutes | **Cooling time:** 2 hours
Equipment: Muffin tin, hand mixer or stand mixer, immersion blender (optional)

If you want a guaranteed crowd-pleasing cupcake for any occasion, this recipe might be my number one recommendation. I have yet to meet someone who doesn't love this dessert duo. With a rich, chocolaty cake base and creamy peanut butter topping, you really can't go wrong.

FOR THE CUPCAKES

½ cup full-fat coconut milk

½ teaspoon white vinegar

1 cup brown rice flour

¾ cup coconut sugar

½ cup almond flour

½ cup unsweetened cocoa powder

1½ teaspoons baking powder

½ teaspoon baking soda

¼ teaspoon sea salt

1 medium ripe banana, mashed

¼ cup melted coconut oil

3 tablespoons maple syrup

1 teaspoon vanilla extract

1. Preheat the oven to 350°F. Line a muffin tin with cupcake liners.

2. In a medium bowl, combine the coconut milk and vinegar. Whisk and set aside.

3. In a large bowl or stand mixer, mix the brown rice flour, coconut sugar, almond flour, cocoa powder, baking powder, baking soda, and salt. Stir to blend.

4. To the bowl with the coconut milk and vinegar, add the mashed banana, melted coconut oil, maple syrup, and vanilla. Whisk until creamy.

5. Pour the wet ingredients into the flour mixture. Beat until a batter forms.

6. Transfer the batter into the cupcake liners, filling each cup about three-quarters of the way full.

7. Bake for 20 to 24 minutes, until a toothpick inserted in the center comes out clean. Immediately transfer the cupcakes to a wire rack (careful, the muffin tin will be hot!) to completely cool, about 2 hours, before frosting.

¾ **cup coconut oil**

¾ **cup palm oil shortening**

½ **cup creamy peanut butter**

⅓ **cup arrowroot starch
   or tapioca flour**

⅛ **teaspoon sea salt**

¼ **cup maple syrup**

1 **teaspoon vanilla extract**

8. To make the peanut butter frosting, in a large bowl, combine the coconut oil and palm oil shortening. Beat with a hand mixer or immersion blender with the whisk tool until fluffy, about 1 minute.

9. Add the peanut butter and beat again until combined, scraping down the sides of the bowl as needed. Add the arrowroot starch and salt, and beat again. Beat in the maple syrup and vanilla.

10. Using a spatula, mix the frosting. Frost the cooled cupcakes immediately, or transfer the frosting to the refrigerator for 10 minutes for a more dense texture.

Storage: Frosted cupcakes can be stored in an airtight container at room temperature for 1 day. If making them in advance, wrap unfrosted cupcakes tightly in plastic wrap, and store at room temperature for up to 3 days. Make the frosting when ready to serve, or store it in an airtight container at room temperature for up to 1 week. Stir before using, and 10 minutes before frosting, place it in the refrigerator for a denser texture, if desired.

Prep tip: The frosting can be easily spread with a spoon or knife. You can also place the frosting in a plastic sandwich bag, cut a small corner off one end, and squeeze to pipe.

Strawberry Cupcakes with Strawberry Frosting

PREP AHEAD • SOY-FREE | **Makes:** 12 cupcakes

Prep time: 20 minutes | **Cook time:** 25 minutes | **Cooling time:** 2 hours 10 minutes
Equipment: Muffin tin, food processor, hand mixer or stand mixer

When it comes to cupcakes, some people like them on the fruity side. If you're in that camp, these cupcakes are for you! Even if that's not normally your thing, I have no doubt that these cupcakes' strawberry sweetness will win you over. Top these cupcakes with an extra strawberry slice for a lovely presentation.

FOR THE CUPCAKES

- ½ cup full-fat coconut milk
- 2 tablespoons freshly squeezed lemon juice (from about ½ lemon)
- 2 cups strawberries, stemmed and halved
- 1½ teaspoons vanilla extract, divided
- 1 cup brown rice flour
- ¾ cup almond flour
- ¾ cup coconut sugar
- 2 tablespoons tapioca flour
- 1½ teaspoons baking powder
- ½ teaspoon baking soda
- ¼ teaspoon sea salt
- 3 tablespoons maple syrup

1. Preheat the oven to 350°F. Line a muffin tin with cupcake liners.

2. In a medium bowl, mix the coconut milk and lemon juice. Whisk and set aside.

3. In a food processor, combine the strawberries with ½ teaspoon of vanilla. Process until puréed, scraping down the sides as needed. Transfer the purée to a small bowl or measuring cup (it should yield about 1 cup).

4. In a large bowl or stand mixer, mix the brown rice flour, almond flour, coconut sugar, tapioca flour, baking powder, baking soda, and salt. Stir to combine.

5. To the bowl with the coconut milk and lemon juice, add ¾ cup of strawberry purée (reserving the rest for the frosting), the remaining 1 teaspoon of vanilla, and maple syrup. Whisk.

6. Pour the wet ingredients into the flour mixture, and beat until a batter forms.

¾ **cup coconut oil**

¾ **cup palm oil shortening**

⅓ **cup arrowroot starch
or tapioca flour**

⅛ **teaspoon sea salt**

¼ **cup maple syrup**

½ **teaspoon vanilla extract**

7. Spoon the batter into the cupcake liners, filling each cup about two-thirds to three-quarters of the way full. Bake for 22 to 24 minutes, or until a toothpick inserted in the center comes out clean. Allow the cupcakes to slightly cool in the muffin tin, 5 to 10 minutes, before transferring them to a wire rack to cool completely before frosting, about 2 hours.

8. To make the strawberry frosting, in a separate large bowl, combine the coconut oil and palm oil shortening. Beat until fluffy, about 1 minute.

9. Add the arrowroot starch and salt, and beat again. Add the maple syrup, reserved strawberry purée, and vanilla, and beat again.

10. Using a spatula, mix the frosting. Frost the cooled cupcakes immediately, or transfer the frosting to the refrigerator for 10 minutes for a more dense texture.

Storage: Frosted cupcakes can be stored in an airtight container at room temperature for 1 day. If making them in advance, wrap unfrosted cupcakes tightly in plastic wrap, and store at room temperature for up to 3 days. Make the frosting when ready to serve, or store it in an airtight container at room temperature for up to 1 week. Stir before using, and 10 minutes before frosting, place it in the refrigerator for a denser texture, if desired.

Prep tip: The frosting can be easily spread with a spoon or knife. You can also place the frosting in a plastic sandwich bag and cut a small corner off one end. Squeeze to pipe.

Mint Chocolate Chip Cupcakes with Peppermint Frosting

PREP AHEAD • SOY-FREE | **Makes:** 10 to 12 cupcakes

Prep time: 20 minutes | **Cook time:** 25 minutes | **Cooling time:** 2 hours
Equipment: Muffin tin, hand mixer or stand mixer, high-speed blender
or food processor (optional), immersion blender (optional)

The mint and chocolate chip combination can be found in many forms (ice cream and cookies, for example), but I love it in these cupcakes. A small serving of peppermint extract gives these chocolate cupcakes a subtle hint of that refreshingly sweet taste.

FOR THE CUPCAKES

½ cup full-fat coconut milk

½ teaspoon white vinegar

1 cup brown rice flour

¾ cup coconut sugar

½ cup almond flour

½ cup unsweetened
cocoa powder

1½ teaspoons baking powder

½ teaspoon baking soda

¼ teaspoon sea salt

1 ripe avocado

3 tablespoons maple syrup

¼ teaspoon vanilla extract

¼ cup melted coconut oil

1 teaspoon peppermint
extract

½ cup dairy-free
chocolate chips

1. Preheat the oven to 350°F. Line a muffin tin with cupcake liners.

2. In a small bowl or measuring cup, mix the coconut milk and vinegar. Whisk and set aside.

3. In a large bowl or stand mixer, mix the brown rice flour, coconut sugar, almond flour, cocoa powder, baking powder, baking soda, and salt. Stir to blend.

4. Transfer the coconut milk mixture to a high-speed blender or food processor. Add the avocado, maple syrup, and vanilla. Blend until creamy. If you don't have a blender or food processor, you can mash the avocado by hand with a fork and whisk everything together in a medium bowl.

5. Pour the coconut milk mixture into the flour mixture. Start beating on medium speed. Add the melted coconut oil and peppermint extract, beating until a batter forms, increasing the speed if needed. Fold in the chocolate chips.

FOR THE PEPPERMINT FROSTING

¾ **cup coconut oil**

¾ **cup palm oil shortening**

⅓ **cup arrowroot starch or tapioca flour**

⅛ **teaspoon sea salt**

¼ **cup plus 2 tablespoons maple syrup**

1 **teaspoon peppermint extract**

6. Spoon the batter into the cupcake liners, filling each cup about three-quarters of the way full. Bake for 22 to 24 minutes, or until a toothpick inserted in the center comes out clean. Immediately transfer the cupcakes to a wire rack (careful, muffin tin will be hot!) to completely cool, about 2 hours, before frosting.

7. To make the peppermint frosting, in a large bowl, mix the coconut oil and palm oil shortening. Beat with a hand mixer or immersion blender with the whisk tool until fluffy, about 1 minute.

8. Add the arrowroot starch and salt, and beat again. Add the maple syrup and peppermint extract, and beat until everything combines, using a spatula to scrape down the sides as needed.

9. Using a spatula, mix the frosting. Frost the cooled cupcakes immediately, or transfer the frosting to the refrigerator for 10 minutes for a denser texture.

Storage: Frosted cupcakes can be stored in an airtight container at room temperature for 1 day. If making them in advance, wrap unfrosted cupcakes tightly in plastic wrap, and store at room temperature for up to 3 days. Make the frosting when ready to serve, or store it in an airtight container at room temperature for up to 1 week. Stir before using, and 10 minutes before frosting, place it in the refrigerator for a denser texture, if desired.

Prep tip: The frosting can be easily spread with a spoon or knife. You can also place the frosting in a plastic sandwich bag and cut a small corner off one end. Squeeze to pipe.

Salted Caramel Cupcakes

PREP AHEAD • SOY-FREE | **Makes:** 10 cupcakes

Prep time: 30 minutes | **Cook time:** 25 minutes | **Cooling time:** 2 hours 10 minutes
Equipment: High-speed blender or food processor, muffin tin,
hand mixer or stand mixer, food thermometer (optional)

The salty-sweet combination is such a delicious trick for your taste buds. You'd be hard pressed not to fall in love with these cupcakes' naturally sweet date caramel sprinkled with large-flake sea salt pieces—and that's not to mention the moist texture. Baking the date caramel into this dessert is one of my favorite ways to use it, and these cupcakes are an amazing way to celebrate any occasion.

FOR THE DATE CARAMEL

2 cups (about 20 large) Medjool dates (with pits)
3 to 4 cups boiling water
1 teaspoon vanilla extract
Pinch sea salt

FOR THE CUPCAKES

½ cup full-fat coconut milk
½ teaspoon white vinegar
1 cup brown rice flour
¾ cup almond flour
¾ cup coconut sugar
2 tablespoons tapioca flour
1½ teaspoons baking powder
½ teaspoon baking soda
¼ teaspoon sea salt
¼ cup maple syrup
1 teaspoon vanilla extract
¼ cup melted coconut oil

1. To make the date caramel, in a medium bowl, soak the dates in boiling water for 20 minutes.

2. Drain the dates, reserving 3 tablespoons of the soaking water. Peel the dates (the skin should easily come off) and remove the pits.

3. In a high-speed blender or food processor, combine the pitted dates, reserved soaking water, vanilla, and salt. Blend for 20 to 30 seconds, scraping down the sides as needed, until creamy. Transfer the mixture to a small bowl and set aside.

4. Preheat the oven to 350°F. Line a muffin tin with cupcake liners.

5. To make the cupcakes, in a separate small bowl or measuring cup, mix the coconut milk and vinegar. Whisk and set aside. In a large bowl or stand mixer, mix the brown rice flour, almond flour, coconut sugar, tapioca flour, baking powder, baking soda, and salt. Stir to blend.

6. Transfer the coconut milk mixture to the blender or food processor. Add half of the date caramel (reserving the rest for the frosting), along with the maple syrup and vanilla. Blend until creamy.

½ cup coconut oil

½ cup palm shortening

3 tablespoons arrowroot
    starch or tapioca flour

¼ cup sea salt, plus
    more for sprinkling

½ cup date caramel
    (reserved from earlier)

¼ cup maple syrup

1 teaspoon vanilla extract

7. Pour the wet ingredients into the flour mixture. Start beating on medium speed, slowly incorporating the melted coconut oil. Continue to beat until a batter forms, increasing the speed as needed.

8. Transfer the batter into the cupcake liners, filling the cups two-thirds to three-quarters of the way full. Bake for 22 to 24 minutes, until the tops are golden brown and a toothpick inserted in the center comes out clean. (If using a food thermometer, the internal temperature should reach 195°F to 200°F.) Allow the cupcakes to slightly cool for 5 to 10 minutes in the muffin tin before transferring them to a wire rack to cool completely before frosting, about 2 hours.

9. To make the frosting, in a large bowl, mix the coconut oil and palm oil shortening. Beat until fluffy, about 1 minute.

10. Add the arrowroot starch and salt, and beat again. Add the reserved date caramel, maple syrup, and vanilla, and beat until everything combines, using a spatula to scrape down the sides as needed.

11. Using a spatula, mix the frosting. Frost the cooled cupcakes immediately, or transfer the frosting to the refrigerator for 10 minutes for a denser texture.

Storage: Frosted cupcakes can be stored in an airtight container at room temperature for 1 day. If making them in advance, wrap unfrosted cupcakes tightly in plastic wrap, and store at room temperature for up to 3 days. Make the frosting when ready to serve, or store it in an airtight container at room temperature for up to 1 week. Stir before using, and 10 minutes before frosting, place it in the refrigerator for a denser texture, if desired.

Ingredient tip: This recipe for date caramel yields about 1 cup. Therefore, about ½ cup should be measured out for the cupcakes, with the remaining ½ cup for the frosting.

Plan-ahead tip: The date caramel can be made up to 4 days in advance. Store in an airtight container in the refrigerator until ready to use.

Apple Upside-Down Cake

PREP AHEAD • SOY-FREE | Serves: 8 to 10

Prep time: 20 minutes | **Cook time:** 55 minutes | **Cooling time:** 2 hours
Equipment: 8-inch round springform cake pan, hand mixer
or stand mixer, food thermometer (optional)

Like a candy apple in cake form, but so much more satisfying. Once you flip
this dish right-side up, you will not be able to resist the sweet and sticky sauce
surrounding the soft-baked apples on top. This dessert has a unique, naturally
moist texture, and you would never know the caramel sauce is vegan.

FOR THE CARAMEL SAUCE

¾ cup coconut sugar
½ cup full-fat coconut milk
½ teaspoon vanilla extract
Pinch sea salt

1. To make the caramel sauce, in a small saucepan over medium-high heat, mix the coconut sugar and coconut milk. Stir to blend. Bring to a boil, stirring occasionally. Reduce the heat to medium-low and simmer until the sauce has thickened and reduced by half, about 10 minutes. Remove the saucepan from the heat and stir in the vanilla and salt. Allow the sauce to cool for at least 10 minutes.

2. Preheat the oven to 350°F. Spray a 8-inch round springform cake pan with cooking spray.

3. To make the cake, in a small bowl, prepare the flax eggs by whisking together the ground flaxseed and water. Set aside for at least 10 minutes.

4. In a medium bowl, mix the coconut milk and vinegar. Whisk and set aside.

5. In a large bowl or stand mixer, mix the brown rice flour, almond flour, coconut sugar, apple pie spice, baking powder, baking soda, and salt. Stir to blend.

6. To the bowl with the coconut milk and vinegar, add the flax eggs, applesauce, maple syrup, and vanilla. Whisk until creamy.

Nonstick cooking spray

2 flax eggs (2 tablespoons
    ground flaxseed and
    4 tablespoons water)

¾ cup full-fat coconut milk or
    unsweetened almond milk

1 teaspoon apple cider vinegar

1¼ cups brown rice flour

1¼ cups almond flour

¾ cup coconut sugar

1 tablespoon apple pie spice
    (or 1½ teaspoons ground
    cinnamon, ¾ teaspoon
    ground nutmeg,
    ½ teaspoon ground
    allspice, and ¼ teaspoon
    ground cardamom)

1½ teaspoons baking powder

½ teaspoon baking soda

¼ teaspoon sea salt

¾ cup unsweetened
    applesauce

¼ cup maple syrup

1 teaspoon vanilla extract

2 tablespoons melted
    coconut oil

2 cups thinly sliced
    apple (about 1 medium
    apple, peeled)

7. Pour the wet ingredients into the flour mixture. Start beating on medium speed, slowly incorporating the melted coconut oil. Increase the speed and continue to beat until a batter forms.

8. Pour the caramel sauce in the bottom of the prepared cake pan. Layer in the sliced apple. Pour the batter on top of the apples.

9. Bake for 50 to 55 minutes, until a toothpick inserted in the center comes out clean or the internal temperature reaches between 200°F and 210°F. Allow the cake to completely cool in the cake pan, about 2 hours. To serve, carefully flip the cake onto a cutting board.

Storage: Wrap the cake tightly in plastic wrap, and store at room temperature for up to 4 days or in the refrigerator for up to 1 week.

New York–Style Cheesecake

GRAIN-FREE • PREP AHEAD • SOY-FREE | **Serves:** 8 to 10

Prep time: 30 minutes, plus 4 to 6 hours to soak
Cook time: 55 minutes | **Cooling time:** 8 hours
Equipment: 8-inch round springform cake pan, hand
mixer or stand mixer, high-speed blender

Someone once asked me if I am a cake person or a pie person. My response: a cheesecake girl through and through! I love any variation of a plant-based cheesecake, but this back-to-basics New York–style rendition will always be my favorite. It tastes so much like the real thing, no one will know it is vegan! Look for Kite Hill brand vegan cream cheese—it's my favorite.

FOR THE CRUST

Nonstick cooking spray
1¼ cups almond flour
¼ cup coconut sugar
**2 tablespoons
    arrowroot starch**
⅓ cup melted coconut oil

1. Preheat the oven to 350°F. Spray an 8-inch round spring-form cake pan with cooking spray.

2. To make the crust, in a large bowl or stand mixer, mix the almond flour, coconut sugar, and arrowroot starch. Stir to blend. Start beating on medium speed, slowly incorporating the melted coconut oil, increasing the speed and beating until a crumbly dough forms. Gather the dough and press it firmly in the bottom of the prepared cake pan (it should feel like damp, coarse sand and should stay compact when you squeeze it).

3. Bake for 10 minutes, then set aside until ready to use.

4. To make the filling, in a high-speed blender, mix the soaked cashews, coconut cream, vegan cream cheese, coconut milk, maple syrup, arrowroot starch, lemon juice, vanilla, and salt. Blend until creamy, using the tamper as needed to get the blender going, until everything is smooth.

FOR THE FILLING

1½ cups raw cashews, soaked in water for at least 4 to 6 hours (or, ideally, overnight), drained and rinsed

1 cup coconut cream (about 2 [5.4-ounce] cans)

1 (8-ounce) package vegan cream cheese, at room temperature

¾ cup full-fat coconut milk

½ cup maple syrup

2 tablespoons arrowroot starch

1 tablespoon freshly squeezed lemon juice

1 teaspoon vanilla extract

¼ teaspoon sea salt

5. Pour the filling into the cake pan with the crust. Bake for 50 to 55 minutes, until the edges have started to turn golden brown and pull away from the sides of the cake pan. (The cheesecake should still "jiggle," and the middle may appear darker but will set as it cools.) Allow the cake to cool at room temperature for at least 2 hours before transferring to the refrigerator for 4 to 6 hours to completely set.

Storage: Store the cheesecake in the refrigerator, covered or uncovered, for up to 5 days.

Plan-ahead tip: The night before, soak the cashews in water, and place the cans of coconut cream upside down in the refrigerator (doing so will allow any liquid to remain at the bottom when turned right-side up, leaving the solidified cream at the top). Reserve the liquid for smoothies or freeze in an ice cube tray for later use.

Chocolate-Cherry Cheesecake

GRAIN-FREE • PREP AHEAD • SOY-FREE | **Serves:** 8 to 10

Prep time: 40 minutes, plus 4 to 6 hours to soak
Cook time: 50 minutes | **Cooling time:** 8 hours 30 minutes
Equipment: 8-inch round springform cake pan, hand
mixer or stand mixer, high-speed blender

With its fudgy filling under a fruity layer, this cheesecake is a sweet treat that seems sinfully delicious but can be fully enjoyed without the guilt. If you love the chocolate-cherry combination, this recipe is right up your alley, a decadent dessert perfect for celebrating Valentine's Day or an anniversary.

FOR THE CRUST

Nonstick cooking spray

1¼ cups almond flour

¼ cup coconut sugar

2 tablespoons
    arrowroot starch

2 tablespoons unsweetened
    cocoa powder

⅓ cup melted coconut oil

1. Preheat the oven to 350°F. Spray an 8-inch round spring-form cake pan with cooking spray.

2. To make the crust, in a large bowl or stand mixer, mix the almond flour, coconut sugar, arrowroot starch, and cocoa powder. Stir to blend. Start beating on medium speed, slowly incorporating the melted coconut oil, increasing the speed and beating until a crumbly dough forms. Gather the dough and press it firmly in the bottom of the prepared cake pan (it should feel like damp, coarse sand and should stay compact when you squeeze it).

3. Bake for 10 minutes, then set aside until ready to use.

4. To make the filling, in a small saucepan, mix the dairy-free chocolate chips and coconut oil. Cook over medium heat until melted, 2 to 3 minutes, stirring frequently (watch carefully to make sure the mixture doesn't burn). Remove from the heat and set aside.

5. In a high-speed blender, mix the soaked cashews, vegan cream cheese, coconut milk, maple syrup, coconut cream, cocoa powder, arrowroot starch, vanilla, and salt. Blend until creamy, using the tamper as needed to get the blender going, until everything is smooth. Add the melted chocolate mixture, and blend again.

½ cup dairy-free
    chocolate chips

3 tablespoons coconut oil,
    softened or melted

1½ cups raw cashews,
    soaked in water for
    at least 4 to 6 hours
    (or, ideally, overnight),
    drained and rinsed

1 (8-ounce) package vegan
    cheese, room temperature

½ cup full-fat coconut milk

½ cup maple syrup

½ cup coconut cream (about
    1 [5.4-ounce] can)

3 tablespoons unsweetened
    cocoa powder

2 tablespoons
    arrowroot starch

1 teaspoon vanilla extract

¼ teaspoon sea salt

FOR THE
CHERRY TOPPING

3 tablespoons coconut oil,
    softened or melted

1½ to 2 cups frozen cherries
    (about 1 [8-ounce] bag)

⅓ cup coconut sugar or
    granulated sugar

1 teaspoon vanilla extract

1 to 2 tablespoons arrowroot
    starch, depending on how
    thick you want the topping

6. Pour the filling into the cake pan with the crust. Bake for 45 to 50 minutes, until the edges have started to turn golden brown and pull away from the sides of the cake pan. (The cheesecake might still "jiggle," and the middle may appear darker but will set as it cools—an inserted toothpick will come out pretty clean.) Allow the cake to cool at room temperature for at least 2 hours before transferring to the refrigerator for 4 to 6 hours or, ideally, overnight to completely set.

7. To make the cherry topping, in a large pot or Dutch oven, heat the coconut oil over medium-high heat. Add the cherries to the pot. Cook for 3 to 5 minutes until thawed, stirring occasionally.

8. Add the coconut sugar and vanilla. Stir to combine. Reduce the heat to low and add the arrowroot starch, stirring vigorously until combined (start with 1 tablespoon of arrowroot starch. If you would like it thicker, add up to 1 additional tablespoon). Cook for about 1 more minute, then remove the pot from the heat, and transfer the cherry mixture to a separate small glass or ceramic bowl to cool for at least 10 to 15 minutes.

9. Pour on top of the chilled cheesecake (while still in the cake pan), and transfer the pan back to the refrigerator for 30 minutes.

Storage: Store the cheesecake in the refrigerator, covered or uncovered, for up to 5 days.

Plan-ahead tip: The night before, soak the cashews in water, and place a can of coconut cream upside down in the refrigerator (doing so will allow any liquid to remain at the bottom when turned right-side up, leaving the solidified cream at the top).

Chocolate Cake with Chocolate Frosting

PREP AHEAD • SOY-FREE | **Serves:** 12 to 16

Prep time: 20 minutes | **Cook time:** 35 minutes | **Cooling time:** 2 hours
Equipment: Two 8-inch round springform cake pans, hand mixer or stand
mixer, immersion blender (optional), food thermometer (optional)

This dessert needs little introduction. If you're a chocolate lover, this is the cake to celebrate any birthday, holiday, or other special occasion. The cake itself is wonderfully moist and sweet (but not overly so), surrounded with a fudge-like frosting that won't set you over the edge. Any of the frosting recipes would pair well with this treat, so have fun playing around with different combinations.

FOR THE CAKE

Nonstick cooking spray

4 flax eggs (4 tablespoons ground flaxseed and 8 tablespoons water)

1 cup full-fat coconut milk or unsweetened almond milk

1 teaspoon white vinegar

1½ cups brown rice flour

1 cup almond flour

¾ cup coconut sugar

½ cup unsweetened cocoa powder

1½ teaspoons baking powder

1 teaspoon baking soda

½ teaspoon sea salt

½ cup pumpkin purée

⅓ cup maple syrup

1 teaspoon vanilla extract

¼ cup melted coconut oil or vegan butter

1. Preheat the oven to 350°F. Spray two 8-inch round springform cake pans with cooking spray.

2. In a small bowl, prepare the flax eggs by whisking together the ground flaxseed and water. Set aside for at least 10 minutes.

3. In a medium bowl, mix the coconut milk and vinegar. Whisk and set aside.

4. In a large bowl or stand mixer, mix the brown rice flour, almond flour, coconut sugar, cocoa powder, baking powder, baking soda, and salt. Stir to blend.

5. To the bowl with the coconut milk and vinegar, add the flax eggs, pumpkin purée, maple syrup, and vanilla. Blend until creamy.

6. Pour the wet ingredients into the flour mixture and start beating on medium speed. Incorporate the melted coconut oil, and continue to beat until a batter forms, increasing the speed as needed. Mix the batter with a spatula to work everything together.

FOR THE CHOCOLATE FROSTING

¾ **cup coconut oil**

¾ **cup palm oil shortening**

½ **cup unsweetened cocoa powder**

¼ **cup arrowroot starch or tapioca flour**

¼ **cup coconut sugar**

⅛ **teaspoon sea salt**

¼ **cup plus 2 tablespoons maple syrup**

1 **teaspoon vanilla extract**

7. Evenly distribute the batter between the prepared cake pans, smoothing on top with a spatula until it reaches the sides. Bake for 30 to 35 minutes, until a toothpick inserted in the center comes out clean or the internal temperature reaches between 200°F and 210°F. Allow the cakes to completely cool in the cake pans before frosting, about 2 hours.

8. To make the chocolate frosting, in a large bowl, mix the coconut oil and palm oil shortening. Beat with a hand mixer or immersion blender with the whisk tool until fluffy, about 1 minute.

9. Add the cocoa powder, arrowroot starch, coconut sugar, and salt, and beat again. Add the maple syrup and vanilla, and beat until everything combines, using a spatula to scrape down the sides as needed.

10. Using a spatula, mix the frosting. Frost the cooled cake immediately, or transfer the frosting to the refrigerator for 10 minutes for a more dense texture. Spread one-third of the frosting on top of one cake. Place the second cake on top, and spread the remaining frosting on top and around the sides.

Storage: Store the frosted cake in a cake keeper at room temperature for up to 4 days; or wrap unfrosted cakes tightly in plastic wrap and store them at room temperature for up to 3 days, then frost when ready to serve. The frosting can be made up to 4 days in advance and stored in an airtight container at room temperature. Stir before using.

Serving tip: If serving on the same day, transfer the frosted cake to the refrigerator for 10 minutes to allow the frosting to set.

Vanilla Cake with Buttercream Frosting

PREP AHEAD • SOY-FREE | Serves: 12 to 16

Prep time: 20 minutes | **Cook time:** 35 minutes | **Cooling time:** 2 hours
Equipment: Two 8-inch round springform cake pans, hand mixer or stand mixer, immersion blender (optional), food thermometer (optional)

Sweet, soft, and moist with a noticeable (but not overpowering) hint of vanilla flavor. That is how I would describe this anything-but-basic cake. It is the perfect versatile dessert to serve on any occasion: birthday, bridal luncheon, or holiday dinner, to name a few.

FOR THE CAKE

Nonstick cooking spray

4 flax eggs (4 tablespoons ground flaxseed and 8 tablespoons water)

¾ cup full-fat coconut milk or unsweetened almond milk

1 teaspoon apple cider vinegar

1½ cups white rice flour or brown rice flour

1½ cups almond flour

¾ cup coconut sugar

2 tablespoons tapioca flour

1½ teaspoons baking powder

1 teaspoon baking soda

½ teaspoon sea salt

½ cup unsweetened applesauce

⅓ cup maple syrup

1 tablespoon vanilla extract

2 tablespoons melted coconut oil

1. Preheat the oven to 350°F. Spray two 8-inch round springform cake pans with cooking spray.

2. In a small bowl, prepare the flax eggs by whisking together the ground flaxseed and water. Set aside for at least 10 minutes.

3. In a medium bowl, mix the coconut milk and vinegar. Whisk and set aside.

4. In a large bowl or stand mixer, mix the white rice flour, almond flour, coconut sugar, tapioca flour, baking powder, baking soda, and salt. Stir to blend.

5. To the bowl with the coconut milk and vinegar, add the flax eggs, applesauce, maple syrup, and vanilla. Whisk until blended.

6. Pour the wet ingredients into the flour mixture, and while beating on medium speed, incorporate the melted coconut oil. Continue to beat, increasing the speed to high if needed, until a batter forms.

¾ cup coconut oil

¾ cup palm oil shortening

⅓ cup arrowroot starch
  or tapioca flour

⅛ teaspoon sea salt

¼ cup plus 2 tablespoons
  maple syrup

2 teaspoons vanilla extract

7. Evenly distribute the batter between the prepared cake pans, smoothing on top with a spatula until it reaches the sides. Bake for 30 to 35 minutes, until a toothpick inserted in the center comes out clean or the internal temperature reaches 200°F. Allow the cakes to completely cool in the cake pans before frosting, about 2 hours.

8. To make the vanilla buttercream frosting, in a large bowl, mix the coconut oil and palm oil shortening. Beat with a hand mixer or immersion blender with the whisk tool until fluffy, about 1 minute.

9. Add the arrowroot starch and salt, and beat again. Add the maple syrup and vanilla, and beat until everything combines, using a spatula to scrape down the sides as needed.

10. Using a spatula, mix the frosting. Frost the cooled cake immediately, or transfer the frosting to the refrigerator for 10 minutes for a denser texture. Spread one-third of the frosting on top of one cake. Place the second cake on top, and spread the remaining frosting on top and around the sides.

Storage: Store the frosted cake in a cake keeper at room temperature for up to 4 days; or wrap unfrosted cakes tightly in plastic wrap and store them at room temperature for up to 3 days, then frost when ready to serve. The frosting can be made up to 4 days in advance and stored in an airtight container at room temperature. Stir before using.

Serving tip: If serving on the same day, transfer the frosted cake to the refrigerator for 10 minutes to allow the frosting to set.

Peanut Butter Cake

PREP AHEAD • SOY-FREE | Serves: 12 to 16

Prep time: 20 minutes | Cook time: 35 minutes | Cooling time: 2 hours
Equipment: Two 8-inch round springform cake pans, hand mixer
or stand mixer, high-speed blender or food processor (optional),
immersion blender (optional), food thermometer (optional)

So often, peanut butter is a part of a pair (for example, peanut butter and jelly or peanut butter and chocolate). But I want to celebrate this classic spread on its own! If you're as big of a peanut butter fan as I am, you're going to love this dessert. Topped with peanut butter frosting, you get a double dose of the good stuff.

FOR THE CAKE

Nonstick cooking spray

3 flax eggs (3 tablespoons ground flaxseed and 6 tablespoons water)

¾ cup full-fat coconut milk or unsweetened almond milk

1 teaspoon apple cider vinegar

1½ cups brown rice flour

1½ cups almond flour

¾ cup coconut sugar

3 tablespoons tapioca flour

1½ teaspoons baking powder

1 teaspoon baking soda

½ teaspoon sea salt

¾ cup creamy all-natural peanut butter

⅓ cup maple syrup

1 teaspoon vanilla extract

2 tablespoons melted coconut oil

1. Preheat the oven to 350°F. Spray two 8-inch round springform cake pans with cooking spray.

2. In a small bowl, prepare the flax eggs by whisking together the ground flaxseed and water. Set aside for at least 10 minutes.

3. In a small bowl or measuring cup, mix the coconut milk and vinegar. Whisk and set aside.

4. In a large bowl or stand mixer, mix the brown rice flour, almond flour, coconut sugar, tapioca flour, baking powder, baking soda, and salt. Stir to blend.

5. Transfer the coconut milk mixture to a high-speed blender or food processor. Add the flax eggs, peanut butter, maple syrup, and vanilla. Blend until creamy. You can also combine everything in a medium bowl and whisk by hand. (Just make sure the peanut butter is really creamy!)

6. Pour the wet ingredients into the flour mixture, and while beating on medium speed, incorporate the melted coconut oil. Continue to beat, increasing the speed as needed, until a batter forms.

¾ **cup coconut oil**

¾ **cup palm oil shortening**

½ **cup creamy peanut butter**

⅓ **cup arrowroot starch
or tapioca flour**

⅛ **teaspoon sea salt**

¼ **cup maple syrup**

1 teaspoon vanilla extract

7. Evenly distribute the batter between the prepared cake pans. (It will be thick! Use a wetted spatula to more easily spread if you need to, smoothing the top until it reaches the sides.) Bake for 30 to 35 minutes, until a toothpick inserted in the center comes out clean or the internal temperature reaches between 200°F and 205°F. Allow the cakes to completely cool in the cake pans, about 2 hours.

8. To make the peanut butter frosting, in a large bowl, mix the coconut oil and palm oil shortening. Beat with a hand mixer or immersion blender with the whisk tool until fluffy, about 1 minute.

9. Add the peanut butter and beat again until combined, scraping down the sides of the bowl as needed. Add the arrowroot starch and salt, and beat again. Beat in the maple syrup and vanilla.

10. Using a spatula, mix the frosting. Frost the cooled cakes immediately, or transfer the frosting to the refrigerator for 10 minutes for a denser texture. Spread one-third of the frosting on top of one cake. Place the second cake on top, and spread the remaining frosting on top and around the sides.

Storage: Store the frosted cake in a cake keeper at room temperature for up to 4 days; or wrap unfrosted cakes tightly in plastic wrap and store them at room temperature for up to 3 days, then frost when ready to serve. The frosting can be made up to 4 days in advance and stored in an airtight container at room temperature. Stir before using.

Serving tip: If serving on the same day, transfer the frosted cake to the refrigerator for 10 minutes to allow the frosting to set.

Chocolate Chip Cookie Cake

PREP AHEAD • SOY-FREE | Serves: 12 to 16

Prep time: 20 minutes | **Cook time:** 35 minutes | **Cooling time:** 2 hours
Equipment: Two 8-inch round springform cake pans, hand mixer
or stand mixer, high-speed blender or food processor (optional),
immersion blender (optional), food thermometer (optional)

The batter for this cake is so reminiscent of chocolate chip cookie dough,
it might take some willpower not to sneak a spoonful before this goes
in the oven! I promise it will be worth the wait, especially when paired
with the vanilla buttercream frosting. Grab a glass of your favorite
dairy-free milk and enjoy a new spin on an American classic.

FOR THE CAKE

Nonstick cooking spray

¾ cup full-fat coconut milk or
   unsweetened almond milk

1 teaspoon white vinegar

1½ cups brown rice flour

1½ cups almond flour

¾ cup coconut sugar

2 tablespoons tapioca flour

1½ teaspoons baking powder

1 teaspoon baking soda

½ teaspoon sea salt

½ cup creamy almond butter

⅓ cup maple syrup

2 teaspoons vanilla extract

¼ cup melted coconut oil

¾ cup dairy-free
   chocolate chips

1. Preheat the oven to 350°F. Spray two 8-inch round spring-form cake pans with cooking spray.

2. In a small bowl, mix the coconut milk and vinegar. Whisk and set aside.

3. In a large bowl or stand mixer, mix the brown rice flour, almond flour, coconut sugar, tapioca flour, baking powder, baking soda, and salt. Stir to blend.

4. Transfer the coconut milk mixture to a high-speed blender or food processor. Add the almond butter, maple syrup, and vanilla. Blend until creamy. You can also combine everything in a medium bowl and whisk by hand. (Just make sure your almond butter is really creamy!)

5. Pour the wet ingredients into the flour mixture, and while beating on medium speed, incorporate the melted coconut oil. Continue to beat, increasing the speed as needed, until a batter forms. Fold in the chocolate chips.

¾ **cup coconut oil**

¾ **cup palm oil shortening**

⅓ **cup arrowroot starch**
   or tapioca flour

⅛ **teaspoon sea salt**

¼ **cup plus 2 tablespoons**
   maple syrup

2 **teaspoons vanilla extract**

6. Evenly distribute the batter between the prepared cake pans. (It will be thick! Use a wetted spatula to more easily spread if you need to, smoothing on top until it reaches the sides.) Bake for 30 to 35 minutes, until a toothpick inserted in the center comes out clean or the internal temperature reaches between 200°F and 205°F. Allow the cakes to completely cool in the pans, about 2 hours.

7. To make the vanilla buttercream frosting, in a large bowl, mix the coconut oil and palm oil shortening. Beat with a hand mixer or immersion blender with the whisk tool until fluffy, about 1 minute.

8. Add the arrowroot starch and salt and beat again. Add the maple syrup and vanilla and beat until everything combines, using a spatula to scrape down the sides as needed.

9. Using a spatula, mix the frosting. Frost the cooled cakes immediately or transfer the frosting to the refrigerator for 10 minutes for a denser texture. Spread one-third of the frosting on top of one cake. Place the second cake on top and add the remaining frosting on top and around the sides.

Storage: Store the frosted cake in a cake keeper at room temperature for up to 4 days; or wrap unfrosted cakes tightly in plastic wrap and store them at room temperature for up to 3 days, then frost when ready to serve. The frosting can be made up to 4 days in advance and stored in an airtight container at room temperature. Stir before using.

Serving tip: If serving on the same day, transfer the frosted cake to the refrigerator for 10 minutes to allow the frosting to set.

Carrot Cake with Vegan Cream Cheese Frosting

PREP AHEAD • SOY-FREE | **Serves:** 12 to 16

Prep time: 30 minutes | **Cook time:** 50 minutes | **Cooling time:** 2 hours
Equipment: Box grater, two 8-inch round springform cake pans, hand mixer
or stand mixer, immersion blender (optional), food thermometer (optional)

I remember the occasion so clearly: It was a random Saturday night during a beach vacation with my best friend's family. After dinner, my best friend's mom presented the most beautiful carrot cake. It was neither a holiday nor anyone's birthday, just a gathering of loved ones to be celebrated. To this day, it is one of those most delicious desserts I have tasted, and this recipe is inspired by (and dedicated to) her.

FOR THE CAKE

Nonstick cooking spray

4 flax eggs (4 tablespoons ground flaxseed and 8 tablespoons water)

¾ cup full-fat coconut milk or unsweetened almond milk

1 teaspoon apple cider vinegar

1½ cups brown rice flour

1½ cups almond flour

¾ cup coconut sugar

3 tablespoons tapioca flour

3 teaspoons ground cinnamon

1½ teaspoons baking powder

1 teaspoon baking soda

½ teaspoon sea salt

¼ teaspoon ground nutmeg (optional)

½ cup unsweetened applesauce

¼ cup maple syrup

¼ cup melted coconut oil

2½ cups grated carrots

½ cup chopped walnuts

1. Preheat the oven to 350°F. Spray two 8-inch round springform cake pans with cooking spray.

2. In a small bowl, prepare the flax eggs by whisking together the ground flaxseed and water. Set aside for at least 10 minutes.

3. In a medium bowl, mix the coconut milk and vinegar. Whisk and set aside.

4. In a large bowl or stand mixer, mix the brown rice flour, almond flour, coconut sugar, tapioca flour, cinnamon, baking powder, baking soda, salt, and nutmeg (if using). Stir to blend.

5. To the bowl with the coconut milk and vinegar, add the flax eggs, applesauce, and maple syrup. Whisk until creamy.

6. Pour the wet ingredients into the flour mixture, and while beating on medium speed, incorporate the melted coconut oil, beating until a batter forms, increasing the speed as needed. Fold in the grated carrots and walnuts.

¾ cup coconut oil

¾ cup palm shortening

⅓ cup vegan cream cheese,
at room temperature (I
suggest Kite Hill brand)

⅓ cup arrowroot starch
or tapioca flour

1 tablespoon coconut sugar
or maple syrup (optional)

⅛ teaspoon sea salt

¼ cup plus 2 tablespoons
maple syrup

1 teaspoon vanilla extract

7. Evenly distribute the batter between the prepared cake pans, smoothing on top with a spatula until it reaches the sides. Bake for 45 to 50 minutes, until a toothpick inserted in the center comes out clean or the internal temperature reaches between 200°F and 205°F. Allow the cakes to completely cool in the cake pans, about 2 hours.

8. To make the vegan cream cheese frosting, in a large bowl, mix the coconut oil and palm oil shortening. Beat with a hand mixer or immersion blender with the whisk tool until fluffy, about 1 minute.

9. Add the vegan cream cheese, and beat again until blended. Add the arrowroot starch, coconut sugar, and salt, and beat again. Add the maple syrup and vanilla, and beat until everything combines, using a spatula to scrape down the sides as needed.

10. Using a spatula, mix the frosting. Frost the cooled cakes immediately, or transfer the frosting to the refrigerator for 10 minutes for a denser texture. Spread one-third of the frosting on top of one cake. Place the second cake on top, and spread the remaining frosting on top and around the sides.

Storage: Store the frosted cake in a cake keeper at room temperature for up to 4 days; or wrap unfrosted cakes tightly in plastic wrap and store them at room temperature for up to 3 days, then frost when ready to serve. The frosting can be made up to 4 days in advance and stored in an airtight container at room temperature. Stir before using.

Serving tip: If serving on the same day, transfer the frosted cake to the refrigerator for 10 minutes to allow the frosting to set.

Coconut Cake

PREP AHEAD • SOY-FREE | Serves: 12 to 16

Prep time: 20 minutes | **Bake time:** 35 minutes | **Cooling time:** 2 hours
Equipment: Two 8-inch round springform cake pans, hand mixer or stand mixer, immersion blender (optional), food thermometer (optional)

Naturally nutty and sweet, this cake is filled with coconut on all fronts: baked right into the batter, folded into the frosting, even sprinkled on top to satisfy your coconut craving. Use plain, shredded, unsweetened coconut, or toast it in order to enhance the flavor.

FOR THE CAKE

Nonstick cooking spray

4 flax eggs (4 tablespoons ground flaxseed and 8 tablespoons water)

¾ cup full-fat coconut milk

1 teaspoon apple cider vinegar

1½ cups brown rice flour

1½ cups almond flour

¾ cup coconut sugar

½ cup shredded unsweetened coconut

2 tablespoons tapioca flour

1½ teaspoons baking powder

1 teaspoon baking soda

½ teaspoon sea salt

½ cup unsweetened applesauce

⅓ cup maple syrup

1 teaspoon vanilla extract

2 tablespoons melted coconut oil

1. Preheat the oven to 350°F. Spray two 8-inch round springform cake pans with cooking spray.

2. In a small bowl, prepare the flax eggs by whisking together the ground flaxseed and water. Set aside for at least 10 minutes.

3. In a medium bowl, mix the coconut milk and vinegar. Whisk and set aside.

4. In a large bowl or stand mixer, combine the brown rice flour, almond flour, coconut sugar, coconut, tapioca flour, baking powder, baking soda, and salt. Stir to blend.

5. To the bowl with the coconut milk and apple cider vinegar, add the applesauce, maple syrup, and vanilla. Whisk until blended.

6. Pour the wet ingredients into the flour mixture and, while beating on medium speed, incorporate the melted coconut oil. Continue to beat, increasing the speed to high as needed, until a batter forms.

¾ **cup coconut oil**

¾ **cup palm oil shortening**

⅓ **cup arrowroot starch
or tapioca flour**

⅛ **teaspoon sea salt**

¼ **cup plus 2 tablespoons
maple syrup**

2 **teaspoons vanilla extract**

1 **cup shredded unsweetened
coconut, plus more for
sprinkling on top (optional)**

7. Evenly distribute the batter between the prepared cake pans, smoothing on top with a spatula until it reaches the sides. Bake for 30 to 35 minutes, until a toothpick inserted in the center comes out clean or the internal temperature reaches between 200°F and 205°F. Allow the cakes to completely cool in the cake pans, at least 2 hours.

8. To make the frosting, in a large bowl, mix the coconut oil and palm oil shortening. Beat with a hand mixer or immersion blender with the whisk tool until fluffy, about 1 minute.

9. Add the arrowroot starch and salt, and beat again. Add the maple syrup and vanilla, and beat until everything combines, using a spatula to blend everything together and scrape down the sides as needed. Fold in the shredded coconut.

10. Frost the cooled cakes immediately, or transfer the frosting to the refrigerator for 10 minutes for a more dense texture. Spread one-third of the frosting on top of one cake. Place the second cake on top, and add the remaining frosting on top and around the sides. Sprinkle some more shredded coconut on the top of the cake (if using).

Storage: Store the frosted cake in a cake keeper at room temperature for up to 4 days; or wrap unfrosted cakes tightly in plastic wrap and store them at room temperature for up to 3 days, then frost when ready to serve. The frosting can be made up to 4 days in advance and stored in an airtight container at room temperature. Stir before using.

Serving tip: If serving on the same day, transfer the frosted cake to the refrigerator for 10 minutes to allow the frosting to set.

German Chocolate Cake

PREP AHEAD • SOY-FREE | **Serves:** 12 to 16

Prep time: 20 minutes | **Cook time:** 35 minutes | **Cooling time:** 2 hours
Equipment: Two 8-inch round springform cake pans, hand mixer or stand mixer, high-speed blender (optional), food thermometer (optional)

What makes a German chocolate cake so unique is the coconut-pecan frosting. Traditionally made with sugar, butter, egg yolks, and evaporated milk, it is not difficult to get close to the real deal using creamy coconut milk and coconut sugar. Rich and decadent, this dessert is perfect for any chocolate lover who wants something a little different.

FOR THE CAKE

Nonstick cooking spray

4 flax eggs (4 tablespoons ground flaxseed and 8 tablespoons water)

1 cup full-fat coconut milk or unsweetened almond milk

1 teaspoon white vinegar

1½ cups brown rice flour

1 cup almond flour

¾ cup coconut sugar

½ cup unsweetened cocoa powder

1½ teaspoons baking powder

1 teaspoon baking soda

½ teaspoon sea salt

½ cup pumpkin purée

⅓ cup maple syrup

1 teaspoon vanilla extract

¼ cup melted coconut oil or melted vegan butter

1. Preheat the oven to 350°F. Spray two 8-inch round springform cake pans with cooking spray.

2. In a small bowl, prepare the flax eggs by whisking together the ground flaxseed and water. Set aside for at least 10 minutes.

3. In a medium bowl, combine the coconut milk and vinegar. Whisk and set aside.

4. In a large bowl or stand mixer, combine the brown rice flour, almond flour, coconut sugar, cocoa powder, baking powder, baking soda, and salt. Stir to blend.

5. To the bowl with the coconut milk and vinegar, add the flax eggs, pumpkin purée, maple syrup, and vanilla. Blend until creamy.

6. Pour the wet ingredients into the flour mixture and start beating on medium speed. Incorporate the melted coconut oil, and continue to beat until a batter forms, increasing the speed as needed. Mix the batter with a spatula to work everything together.

1 (13.5-ounce) can full-fat
   coconut milk (or 1½ cups
   dairy-free milk of choice)

1 teaspoon vanilla extract

1 cup coconut sugar

1½ tablespoons
   arrowroot starch

1¼ cups shredded coconut

1 cup chopped pecans

7. Evenly distribute the batter between the prepared cake pans, smoothing on top with a spatula until it reaches the sides. Bake for 30 to 35 minutes, until a toothpick inserted in the center comes out clean or the internal temperature reaches between 200°F and 205°F. Allow the cakes to completely cool in the cake pans, about 2 hours.

8. To make the frosting, in a medium saucepan over medium heat, mix the coconut milk and the vanilla, and bring to a boil. Whisk in the coconut sugar, and continue to cook for 1 to 2 more minutes. Add the arrowroot starch, whisking vigorously by hand and breaking up any clumps. (If you have a high-speed blender, transfer the mixture, blend until smooth, then transfer it back to the saucepan.) Reduce the heat to medium low, and simmer for another minute. Remove the saucepan from the heat, and stir in the shredded coconut and chopped pecans. Allow the mixture to cool for 10 minutes.

9. Once the cakes have cooled, spread half of the frosting on top of one cake. Place the second cake on top, and spread the remaining frosting on top.

Storage: The frosted cake will stay fresh in a cake keeper at room temperature for up to 4 days. You can also wrap unfrosted cakes tightly in plastic wrap and keep them at room temperature for up to 3 days, then frost when ready to serve. The frosting can also be made in advance and stored in an airtight container or mason jar at room temperature for up to 3 days.

Serving tip: You can frost the cake when the frosting is still warm and serve immediately or once cooled to room temperature if serving on the same day. Otherwise, allow the frosting to cool to room temperature before following the storage notes.

Hummingbird Cake with Vegan Cream Cheese Frosting

PREP AHEAD • SOY-FREE | **Serves:** 12 to 16

Prep time: 20 minutes | **Cook time:** 55 minutes | **Cooling time:** 2 hours
Equipment: Two 8-inch round springform cake pans, hand mixer or stand mixer, immersion blender (optional), food thermometer (optional)

The unique trifecta of pineapple, banana, and pecans makes this Southern classic a favorite among my friends and family.

FOR THE CAKE

Nonstick cooking spray

4 flax eggs (4 tablespoons ground flaxseed and 8 tablespoons water)

¾ cup full-fat coconut milk or unsweetened almond milk

1 teaspoon white vinegar or apple cider vinegar

1½ cups brown rice flour

1½ cups almond flour

¾ cup coconut sugar

2 tablespoons tapioca flour

1½ teaspoons baking powder

1 teaspoon baking soda

½ teaspoon sea salt

⅓ cup maple syrup

1 teaspoon vanilla extract

1 (14-ounce) can crushed pineapple, drained

¾ cup mashed ripe banana

¼ cup melted coconut oil

¾ cup roughly chopped pecans

1. Preheat the oven to 350°F. Spray two 8-inch round springform cake pans with cooking spray.

2. In a small bowl, prepare the flax eggs by whisking together the ground flaxseed and water. Set aside for at least 10 minutes.

3. In a medium bowl, mix the coconut milk and vinegar. Whisk and set aside.

4. In a large bowl or stand mixer, mix the brown rice flour, almond flour, coconut sugar, tapioca flour, baking powder, baking soda, and salt. Stir to blend.

5. To the bowl with the coconut milk and vinegar, add the flax eggs, maple syrup, and vanilla. Whisk. Add the pineapple and mashed banana, whisking again until everything combines.

6. Pour the wet ingredients into the flour mixture. While beating on medium speed, incorporate the melted coconut oil, beating until a batter forms, increasing the speed as needed. Fold in the chopped pecans.

7. Divide the batter evenly between the prepared cake pans. Bake for 50 to 55 minutes, until the edges are golden brown and a toothpick inserted in the center comes out clean. The center of the cakes should feel "spongy" to the touch, and

¾ cup coconut oil

¾ cup palm shortening

⅓ cup vegan cream cheese,
at room temperature (I
suggest Kite Hill brand)

⅓ cup arrowroot starch
or tapioca flour

1 tablespoon coconut sugar
or maple syrup (optional)

⅛ teaspoon sea salt

¼ cup plus 2 tablespoons
maple syrup

1 teaspoon vanilla extract

the internal temperature should reach between 200°F and
205°F. Allow the cakes to completely cool in the cake pans,
about 2 hours.

8. To make the vegan cream cheese frosting, in a large bowl,
mix the coconut oil and palm oil shortening. Beat with a hand
mixer or immersion blender with the whisk tool until fluffy,
about 1 minute.

9. Add the vegan cream cheese, and beat again until
blended. Add the arrowroot starch, coconut sugar (if using),
and salt, and beat again. Add the maple syrup and vanilla,
and beat until everything combines, using a spatula to scrape
down the sides as needed.

10. Using a spatula, mix the frosting. Frost the cooled cakes
immediately, or transfer the frosting to the refrigerator for
10 minutes for a denser texture. Spread one-third of the
frosting on top of one cake. Place the second cake on top, and
spread the remaining frosting on top and around the sides.

Storage: The frosted cake will stay fresh in a cake keeper
at room temperature for up to 4 days. You can also wrap
unfrosted cakes tightly in plastic wrap and keep them at room
temperature for up to 3 days, then frost when ready to serve.
The frosting can be made up to 4 days in advance and stored
in an airtight container or mason jar at room temperature.
Give it a good stir before using, as separation might occur.

Prep tip: While you prepare the flax eggs and milk-
vinegar mixture at the start, place the pineapple in a
fine-mesh strainer to drain.

Serving tip: If serving on the same day, transfer the
frosted cake to the refrigerator for 10 minutes to allow the
frosting to set.

Vegan Mascarpone Berry Layer Cake

PREP AHEAD • SOY-FREE | **Serves:** 12 to 16

Prep time: 30 minutes, plus 6 to 8 hours to soak
Cook time: 35 minutes | **Cooling time:** 2 hours
Equipment: High-speed blender, hand mixer or stand mixer, two 8-inch
round springform cake pans, food thermometer (optional)

Traditional mascarpone is known as an "Italian cream cheese." With a
sweet and buttery texture, there is no wonder it is a long-standing delicacy.
Creating a dairy-free version takes some imagination, but I found blending
vanilla cashew cream and coconut whipped cream comes pretty close.

FOR THE VANILLA CASHEW CREAM

2 cups raw whole cashews,
  soaked in water for
  at least 6 to 8 hours
  (or, ideally, overnight),
  drained and rinsed
½ cup unsweetened almond
  milk or dairy-free milk
¼ cup maple syrup
1 teaspoon vanilla extract

FOR THE COCONUT WHIPPED CREAM

1 cup coconut cream (about
  2 [5.4-ounce] cans)
1 tablespoon maple syrup
½ teaspoon vanilla extract

1. To make the vanilla cashew cream, in a high-speed blender, combine the soaked cashews, almond milk, maple syrup, and vanilla. Blend on high until creamy, scraping down the sides as needed. Transfer to a medium bowl.

2. To make the coconut whipped cream, place a separate medium bowl in the freezer for 5 to 10 minutes.

3. Spoon the coconut cream into the chilled bowl, draining any coconut water. Use a hand mixer to beat the coconut cream on high speed until fluffy, about 1 minute.

4. Add the maple syrup and vanilla. Beat for 30 seconds.

5. Transfer the coconut whipped cream into the bowl with the vanilla cashew cream, mix well, and refrigerate to chill. This is the vegan mascarpone

6. To make the cake, preheat the oven to 350°F. Spray two 8-inch round springform cake pans with cooking spray.

7. In a small bowl, prepare the flax eggs by whisking together the ground flaxseed and water. Set aside for at least 10 minutes.

8. In another medium bowl, combine the coconut milk and vinegar. Whisk and set aside.

FOR THE CAKE

Nonstick cooking spray

4 flax eggs (4 tablespoons ground flaxseed and 8 tablespoons water)

¾ cup full-fat coconut milk or unsweetened almond milk

1 teaspoon apple cider vinegar

1½ cups brown rice flour

1½ cups almond flour

¾ cup coconut sugar

3 tablespoons tapioca flour

1½ teaspoons baking powder

1 teaspoon baking soda

½ teaspoon sea salt

¾ cup unsweetened applesauce

⅓ cup maple syrup

1 teaspoon vanilla extract

2 tablespoons melted coconut oil

3 cups fresh berries of choice, for decoration

9. In a large bowl or stand mixer, combine the brown rice flour, almond flour, coconut sugar, tapioca flour, baking powder, baking soda, and salt. Stir to blend.

10. To the bowl with the coconut milk and vinegar, add the flax eggs, applesauce, maple syrup, and vanilla. Whisk until creamy.

11. Pour the wet ingredients into the flour mixture. While beating on medium speed, incorporate the melted coconut oil, increasing the speed as needed, until a batter forms.

12. Evenly distribute the batter between the prepared cake pans, smoothing the top with a spatula until it reaches the sides. Bake for 30 to 35 minutes, until the edges are a slight golden brown and a toothpick inserted in the center comes out clean or the internal temperature reaches between 200°F and 205°F. Allow the cakes to completely cool in the cake pans, about 2 hours.

13. Spread half of the vegan mascarpone on top of one cake, and place the second cake on top. Spread the remaining mascarpone on top. Decorate with the fresh berries.

Storage: The frosted cake will stay fresh in a cake keeper at room temperature for up to 4 days. You can also wrap unfrosted cakes tightly in plastic wrap and keep them at room temperature for up to 3 days, then make the mascarpone when ready to serve.

Plan-ahead tip: Both the vanilla cashew cream and coconut whipped cream can be made in advance, but I recommend no more than 1 or 2 days ahead of time to maintain freshness. Otherwise, the night before you want to make the mascarpone, soak the cashews overnight (for the cashew cream), and place the two cans of coconut cream in the refrigerator upside down (for the whipped cream).

Almond Bundt Cake

PREP AHEAD • SOY-FREE | **Serves:** 12 to 16

Prep time: 15 minutes | **Cook time:** 45 minutes | **Cooling time:** 2 hours
Equipment: 12-cup Bundt pan, hand mixer or stand mixer, food thermometer (optional)

There is something so beautiful yet simple about a Bundt cake. Interestingly, "Bundt cake" is not tethered to a particular recipe; it just describes the distinctive design created by the ring-shaped pan. Enjoy this sweet and easy-to-make version, which is delicious whether on its own, sprinkled with some powdered sugar and/or sliced almonds, or topped with vanilla icing (see Sugar Cookies with Vanilla Icing, page 68). While this cake might not rise like its non-vegan counterparts, the shape and taste are just as great.

Nonstick cooking spray

3 flax eggs (3 tablespoons ground flaxseed and 6 tablespoons water)

¾ cup full-fat coconut milk

1 teaspoon apple cider vinegar

2½ cups almond flour

¾ cup coconut sugar

½ cup brown rice flour

2 teaspoons baking powder

½ teaspoon baking soda

¼ teaspoon sea salt

¾ cup unsweetened applesauce

⅓ cup maple syrup

1 teaspoon vanilla extract

2 tablespoons melted coconut oil

1. Preheat the oven to 350°F. Liberally spray a 12-cup Bundt pan with cooking spray.

2. In a small bowl, prepare the flax eggs by whisking together the ground flaxseed and water. Set aside for at least 10 minutes.

3. In a medium bowl, mix the coconut milk and vinegar. Whisk and set aside.

4. In a large bowl or stand mixer, mix the almond flour, coconut sugar, brown rice flour, baking powder, baking soda, and salt. Stir to blend.

5. To the bowl with the coconut milk and vinegar, add the flax eggs, applesauce, maple syrup, and vanilla. Whisk until creamy.

6. Pour the wet ingredients into the flour mixture. While beating on medium speed, incorporate the melted coconut oil, beating until a batter forms, increasing the speed as needed.

7. Transfer the batter to the prepared Bundt pan. Bake for 40 to 45 minutes, until the edges are golden brown and a toothpick inserted in the center comes out clean or the internal temperature reaches between 200°F and 210°F. Allow the cake to completely cool in the pan, about 2 hours.

Storage: Wrap the cake or individual slices in plastic wrap, and store at room temperature for up to 4 days or in the refrigerator for up to 1 week. Bring the cake to room temperature before serving.

Prep tip: If you don't have a Bundt pan, you can use a loaf pan, but cook time will vary.

Serving tip: Remove the cake by flipping it upside down on a cutting board. Slice sections of desired size.

Chocolate Soufflé

GRAIN-FREE OPTION • NUT-FREE OPTION • SOY-FREE | Serves: 2

Prep time: 10 minutes | **Cook time:** 20 minutes | **Cooling time:** 5 minutes
Equipment: Two 6-ounce ramekins, hand mixer or stand mixer

A delicious dessert for two, this chocolate soufflé is such a sweet ending to a Valentine's Day or anniversary dinner. While the recipe makes two portions, it can easily be doubled (or tripled) to feed more people. Grab a spoon and savor just the right amount of this perfectly portioned rich, chocolaty treat.

Nonstick cooking spray

½ cup dairy-free chocolate chips

3 tablespoons coconut oil, softened or melted

1 cup almond flour, white rice flour, or brown rice flour

¼ cup arrowroot starch

¼ cup coconut sugar

¼ cup unsweetened cocoa powder

½ teaspoon baking powder

¼ teaspoon sea salt

½ cup full-fat coconut milk or unsweetened almond milk

¼ cup maple syrup

½ teaspoon white vinegar

½ teaspoon vanilla extract

1. Preheat the oven to 375°F. Spray two 6-ounce ramekins with cooking spray.

2. In a small saucepan, mix the chocolate chips and coconut oil. Cook over medium heat until melted, 2 to 3 minutes, stirring frequently (watch carefully to make sure the mixture doesn't burn). Remove from the heat and set aside.

3. In a large bowl or stand mixer, mix the almond flour, arrowroot starch, coconut sugar, cocoa powder, baking powder, and salt. Stir to blend, making sure to break up any clumps.

4. In a small bowl, whisk together the coconut milk, maple syrup, vinegar, and vanilla. Add the melted chocolate mixture, and whisk again.

5. Pour the wet ingredients into the flour mixture. Beat until a batter forms. Divide the batter evenly between the prepared ramekins, filling each to the top.

6. Bake for 15 to 18 minutes, until a crust forms on the top that is still slightly soft to the touch. Allow the soufflés to cool for 5 minutes. Serve warm.

Tiramisu

PREP AHEAD • SOY-FREE | **Serves:** 16 to 20

Prep time: 1 hour, plus 6 to 8 hours to soak
Cook time: 15 minutes | **Cooling time:** 1 hour
Equipment: High-speed blender, hand mixer or stand
mixer, baking sheet, 9-by-13-inch baking dish

The pieces to this multilayered and lavish dessert fit together so deliciously. The sweet and spongy sheet cake is layered with a vegan mascarpone filling and topped with a mocha-flavored sauce. While this tiramisu might be more time-consuming than other desserts, if you're a fan of the traditional Italian delicacy, it will be worth it!

FOR THE VANILLA CASHEW CREAM

2 cups raw whole cashews, soaked in water for at least 6 to 8 hours (ideally, overnight), drained and rinsed
½ cup unsweetened almond milk or dairy-free milk
¼ cup maple syrup
1 teaspoon vanilla extract

FOR THE COCONUT WHIPPED CREAM

1 cup coconut cream (about 2 [5.4-ounce] cans)
1 tablespoon maple syrup
½ teaspoon vanilla extract

1. To make the vanilla cashew cream, in a high-speed blender, mix the soaked cashews, almond milk, maple syrup, and vanilla. Blend on high until creamy, scraping down the sides as needed. Transfer to a medium bowl.

2. To make the coconut whipped cream, place a separate medium bowl in the freezer for 5 to 10 minutes.

3. Spoon the coconut cream into the chilled bowl, draining any coconut water. Use a hand mixer to beat the coconut cream on high speed until fluffy, about 1 minute.

4. Add the maple syrup and vanilla. Beat again for 30 seconds.

5. Transfer the coconut whipped cream into the bowl with the vanilla cashew cream, mix well, and refrigerate to chill. This is the vegan mascarpone.

(Continued)

FOR THE SHEET CAKE

2 flax eggs (2 tablespoons ground flaxseed and 4 tablespoons water)

2 cups brown rice flour or gluten-free all-purpose flour

1 cup almond flour

¾ cup coconut sugar or granulated sugar

2 teaspoons baking powder

1 teaspoon baking soda

½ teaspoon sea salt

1 cup full-fat coconut milk or unsweetened almond milk

¼ cup maple syrup

¼ cup melted coconut oil

1 teaspoon vanilla extract

FOR THE SAUCE

¾ cup full-fat coconut milk or unsweetened almond milk

½ cup unsweetened cocoa powder, plus more for dusting, if desired

½ cup coconut sugar or granulated sugar

¼ cup brewed and cooled coffee (with or without caffeine; optional)

1 teaspoon vanilla extract

¼ teaspoon sea salt

6. Preheat the oven to 350°F. Line a baking sheet with parchment paper. (I recommend a 15-by-10-inch half sheet pan.)

7. To make the sheet cake, in another medium bowl, prepare the flax eggs by whisking together the ground flaxseed and water. Set aside for at least 10 minutes.

8. In a large bowl or stand mixer, combine the brown rice flour, almond flour, coconut sugar, baking powder, baking soda, and salt. Stir to blend.

9. To the bowl with the flax eggs, add the coconut milk, maple syrup, melted coconut oil, and vanilla. Whisk until creamy.

10. Pour the wet ingredients into the flour mixture. Beat until a batter forms. Transfer the batter to the prepared baking sheet, using a wetted spatula to spread evenly (it's fine if it doesn't reach the sides). Bake for 15 minutes, or until the edges are golden brown and a toothpick inserted in the center comes out clean. Allow the cake to cool on the baking sheet for at least 1 hour.

11. Once cooled, cut the sheet cake in half and then into 2-by-4-inch rectangles. Lay half of the rectangles on the bottom of a 9-by-13-inch baking dish.

12. To make the sauce, in a small saucepan over medium-high heat, combine the coconut milk, cocoa powder, coconut sugar, and coffee (if using). Whisk vigorously to blend, and bring to a boil, stirring occasionally.

13. Reduce the heat to medium-low, and continue to cook until slightly thickened, 5 to 7 minutes. Whisk in the vanilla and salt. Remove from the heat and allow to cool slightly, about 5 minutes. If a dark film forms on the top, this is normal; just whisk it away.

14. Pour half of the sauce on top of the cake in the baking dish, spreading evenly with a spatula if needed. Spread half of the vegan mascarpone on top. Layer the remaining sheet cake sections, remaining sauce, and remaining mascarpone. Dust with cocoa powder, if desired.

Storage: Cover the baking dish tightly with plastic wrap, and store in the refrigerator for up to 3 days.

Serving tip: This tiramisu can be enjoyed immediately or chilled. To serve it chilled, transfer the baking dish to the refrigerator for at least 2 hours and up to 8 hours, but I suggest allowing it to sit at room temperature for 30 minutes before serving.

Plan-ahead tip: The day before, make the vanilla cashew cream and coconut whipped cream. This will allow for a much shorter preparation time. The cashews will need to be soaked ahead of time as well.

Chocolate-Avocado Mousse Pie, page 136

CHAPTER SIX

PIES AND TARTS

Blueberry Pie

GRAIN-FREE • PREP AHEAD • SOY-FREE | **Serves:** 8 to 10

Prep time: 20 minutes, plus 30 minutes to chill
Cook time: 50 minutes | **Cooling time:** 2 hours
Equipment: Hand mixer or stand mixer, 9-inch pie plate, rolling pin

Because my niece always asks for a fruit pie of some sort, I make this blueberry-filled confection for her. The first time she tried it, I reassured her that it is delicious enough for dessert but nutritious enough to eat for breakfast (which I often do). She looked at me with a skeptical eye, but after one bite, I could see the satisfied smile spread across her face. I can say with confidence that this pie will please even your pickiest of eaters.

FOR THE CRUST

1¾ cups almond flour

¼ cup tapioca flour or arrowroot starch

3 tablespoons coconut sugar

2 teaspoons ground cinnamon

¼ teaspoon sea salt

¼ cup melted coconut oil

¼ cup maple syrup

1 teaspoon vanilla extract

1 teaspoon apple cider vinegar

Nonstick cooking spray

1. To make the crust, in a large bowl or stand mixer, mix the almond flour, tapioca flour, coconut sugar, cinnamon, and salt, using your fingers or the back of a wooden spoon to break up clumps as needed.

2. In a medium bowl, mix the melted coconut oil, maple syrup, vanilla, and vinegar. Whisk until creamy.

3. Pour the wet ingredients into the flour mixture, and beat until a crumbly dough forms. Use your hands to gather the dough into a ball. Wrap the dough tightly in plastic wrap, and refrigerate for 30 minutes.

4. While the dough chills, preheat the oven to 350°F. Spray a 9-inch pie plate with cooking spray.

5. Place the ball of dough between two sheets of parchment paper. Using a rolling pin, roll it out to ⅛ to ¼ inch thick. Flip the flattened dough across the prepared pie plate, using your fingers to press it into the bottom, fix any cracks, and seal around the edges.

6. Prebake the crust for 10 minutes, then set aside until ready to use.

¼ cup coconut oil or vegan butter

4 cups frozen blueberries

½ cup coconut sugar or granulated sugar

Juice of ½ lemon

1 teaspoon vanilla extract

2 tablespoons arrowroot starch

FOR THE
CRUMBLE TOPPING

1 cup almond flour or other gluten-free, grain-free flour

¼ cup coconut sugar

⅓ cup cold vegan butter, cut into 1-inch pieces

7. To make the filling, in a large pot or Dutch oven, heat the coconut oil over medium-high heat. Add the blueberries to the pot, and cook for 5 to 7 minutes, until thawed, stirring occasionally.

8. Add the coconut sugar, lemon juice, and vanilla, and stir to combine. Add the arrowroot starch, and stir again. Reduce the heat to medium low and simmer for 7 to 10 more minutes, stirring occasionally, until the mixture has reduced and thickened. Transfer the blueberry mixture to the pie plate with the prebaked crust. Set aside.

9. To make the crumble topping, in another medium bowl, mix the almond flour and coconut sugar. Stir to blend. Add the vegan butter, and use your hands to mix and massage it into the flour mixture until a crumbly dough forms. Sprinkle the crumble over the blueberry mixture.

10. Bake for 20 to 24 minutes, until the crust edges and crumble have started to turn golden brown. Allow the pie to completely cool at room temperature, about 2 hours.

Storage: Cover the pie with aluminum foil or plastic wrap, and store at room temperature for up to 3 days or in the refrigerator for up to 5 days.

Prep tip: To reduce preparation time, start making the filling while the crust prebakes. You can make the crumble topping while the blueberry mixture simmers in the pot.

Serving tip: Serve after cooling to room temperature, or transfer the pie to the refrigerator for 4 to 6 hours (or, ideally, overnight) to completely set. The pie is just as delicious served chilled.

Pumpkin Pie

GRAIN-FREE • PREP AHEAD • SOY-FREE | **Serves:** 8 to 10

Prep time: 20 minutes, plus 30 minutes to chill
Cook time: 50 minutes | **Cooling time:** 10 hours
Equipment: Hand mixer or stand mixer, 9-inch pie plate,
rolling pin, high-speed blender or food processor

Years ago, I was assigned dessert for Thanksgiving dinner. Of course, I immediately decided on a pumpkin pie, and it was actually the very first vegan baked good I ever made. While I have made some tweaks to the recipe since, I continue to contribute this dish each year. It is one of my favorite desserts, and I am so excited to share it with you. I suggest pairing it with coconut whipped cream (see Mississippi Mud Pie with Coconut Whipped Cream, page 154).

FOR THE CRUST

1¾ cups almond flour

¼ cup tapioca flour or arrowroot starch

3 tablespoons coconut sugar

2 teaspoons ground cinnamon

¼ teaspoon sea salt

¼ cup melted coconut oil

¼ cup maple syrup

1 teaspoon vanilla extract

1 teaspoon apple cider vinegar

Nonstick cooking spray

1. To make the crust, in a large bowl or stand mixer, mix the almond flour, tapioca flour, coconut sugar, cinnamon, and salt, using your fingers or the back of a wooden spoon to break up clumps as needed.

2. In a medium bowl, mix the melted coconut oil, maple syrup, vanilla, and vinegar. Whisk until creamy.

3. Pour the wet ingredients into the flour mixture, and beat until a crumbly dough forms. Use your hands to gather the dough into a ball. Wrap the dough tightly in plastic wrap, and refrigerate for 30 minutes.

4. While the dough chills, preheat the oven to 350°F. Spray a 9-inch pie plate with cooking spray.

½ cup full-fat coconut milk

⅓ cup maple syrup

2½ cups pumpkin purée
(about 1½ [15-ounce]
cans pure pumpkin)

½ cup coconut sugar

¼ cup arrowroot starch

2 teaspoons pumpkin
pie spice

1 teaspoon ground cinnamon

1 teaspoon ground ginger

1 teaspoon vanilla extract

¼ teaspoon sea salt

5. Place the ball of dough between two sheets of parchment paper. Using a rolling pin, roll it out to ⅛ to ¼ inch thick. Flip the flattened dough across the prepared pie plate, using your fingers to press it into the bottom, fix any cracks, and seal around the edges. Place the pie plate in the refrigerator until ready to use.

6. To make the filling, in a high-speed blender or food processor, combine the coconut milk, maple syrup, pumpkin purée, coconut sugar, arrowroot starch, pumpkin pie spice, cinnamon, ginger, vanilla, and salt. Blend until creamy.

7. Transfer the pumpkin mixture to the prepared crust. Bake for 45 to 50 minutes, until the edges are golden brown and the filling looks set (a toothpick inserted in the center should come out clean). Allow the pie to completely cool, about 2 hours. Transfer to the refrigerator for at least 6 to 8 hours or, ideally, overnight to completely set.

Storage: Cover the pie with aluminum foil, and store in the refrigerator for up to 3 days. Serve chilled.

Prep tip: When combining the filling ingredients in a high-speed blender or food processor, add the liquid ingredients first. This will make for smoother processing.

Oat-Crumble Cherry Pie

GRAIN-FREE OPTION • PREP AHEAD • SOY-FREE | Serves: 8 to 10

Prep time: 20 minutes, plus 30 minutes to chill
Cook time: 50 minutes | **Cooling time:** 2 hours
Equipment: Hand mixer or stand mixer, 9-inch pie plate, rolling pin

This pie is a prime example of how less is more. You won't need much to create this classic dessert, which really allows the sweet cherry taste to shine through. While cherries are in the height of their season in the spring and summer months, using frozen cherries (which I keep in my freezer all year round) enables you to enjoy this dish at any time.

FOR THE CRUST

1¾ cups almond flour

¼ cup tapioca flour or arrowroot starch

3 tablespoons coconut sugar

2 teaspoons ground cinnamon

¼ teaspoon sea salt

¼ cup melted coconut oil

¼ cup maple syrup

1 teaspoon vanilla extract

1 teaspoon apple cider vinegar

Nonstick cooking spray

FOR THE FILLING

¼ cup coconut oil or vegan butter

4 to 5 cups frozen cherries

½ cup coconut sugar or granulated sugar

Juice of ½ lemon

1 teaspoon vanilla extract

2 tablespoons arrowroot starch

1. To make the crust, in a large bowl or stand mixer, mix the almond flour, tapioca flour, coconut sugar, cinnamon, and salt, using your fingers or the back of a wooden spoon to break up clumps as needed.

2. In a medium bowl, mix the melted coconut oil, maple syrup, vanilla, and vinegar. Whisk until creamy.

3. Pour the wet ingredients into the flour mixture, and beat until a crumbly dough forms. Use your hands to gather the dough into a ball. Wrap the dough tightly in plastic wrap, and refrigerate for 30 minutes.

4. While the dough chills, preheat the oven to 350°F. Spray a 9-inch pie plate with cooking spray.

5. Place the ball of dough between two sheets of parchment paper. Using a rolling pin, roll it out to ⅛ to ¼ inch thick. Flip the flattened dough across the prepared pie plate, using your fingers to press it into the bottom, fix any cracks, and seal around the edges.

6. Prebake the crust for 10 minutes, then set aside until ready to use.

FOR THE CRUMBLE TOPPING

1 cup gluten-free oats or almond flour

½ cup coconut flour

⅓ cup coconut sugar

2 teaspoons ground cinnamon

¾ cup cold vegan butter, cut into 1-inch pieces

7. To make the filling, in a large pot or Dutch oven, heat the coconut oil over medium-high heat. Add the cherries to the pot. Cook 3 to 5 minutes, until thawed, stirring occasionally.

8. Add the coconut sugar, lemon juice, and vanilla, and stir to combine. Add the arrowroot starch, and stir again. Reduce the heat to medium low and simmer for 7 to 10 more minutes, until the mixture has reduced and thickened. Transfer the cherry mixture to the pie plate with the pre-baked crust.

9. To make the crumble topping, in another large bowl, mix the oats, coconut flour, coconut sugar, and cinnamon. Stir to blend. Add the vegan butter and use your hands to mix and massage it into the oat mixture until a crumble forms. Sprinkle the crumble topping over the pie.

10. Bake for 20 to 24 minutes, until the crumble turns golden brown and the cherry mixture bubbles. Allow the pie to cool completely in the pie plate, at least 2 hours.

Storage: Cover the pie with aluminum foil or plastic wrap, and store at room temperature for up to 3 days or in the refrigerator for up to 5 days.

Prep tip: To reduce preparation time, start making the filling while the crust prebakes. You can make the crumble topping while the cherry mixture simmers in the pot.

Serving tip: Serve after cooling to room temperature, or transfer the pie to the refrigerator for 4 to 6 hours (or, ideally, overnight) to completely set. The pie is just as delicious served chilled.

Chocolate-Avocado Mousse Pie

GRAIN-FREE • PREP AHEAD • SOY-FREE | Serves: 8 to 10

Prep time: 20 minutes, plus 30 minutes to chill
Cook time: 20 minutes | **Cooling time:** 12 hours
Equipment: Hand mixer or stand mixer, 9-inch pie plate,
rolling pin, high-speed blender or food processor

Combining ripe bananas and avocado creates a silky and sweet dessert that goes perfectly in pie. With a crispy crust and creamy, pudding-like filling, I would not be surprised if this became one of your new favorites. While the avocado contributes to the texture, you really can't taste it, and you would never know it is packed with nutrients. The chocolate flavor and natural sweetness shine through.

FOR THE CRUST

1¾ cups almond flour

¼ cup tapioca flour or
   arrowroot starch

3 tablespoons coconut sugar

2 tablespoons unsweetened
   cocoa powder (optional)

¼ teaspoon sea salt

¼ cup melted coconut oil

¼ cup maple syrup

1 teaspoon vanilla extract

1 teaspoon apple cider vinegar

Nonstick cooking spray

1. To make the crust, in a large bowl or stand mixer, mix the almond flour, tapioca flour, coconut sugar, cocoa powder (if using), and salt, using your fingers or the back of a wooden spoon to break up clumps as needed.

2. In a medium bowl, mix the melted coconut oil, maple syrup, vanilla, and vinegar. Whisk until creamy.

3. Pour the wet ingredients into the flour mixture, and beat until a crumbly dough forms. Use your hands to gather the dough into a ball. Wrap the dough tightly in plastic wrap, and refrigerate for 30 minutes.

4. While the dough chills, preheat the oven to 350°F. Spray a 9-inch pie plate with cooking spray.

5. Place the ball of dough between two sheets of parchment paper. Using a rolling pin, roll it out to ⅛ to ¼ inch thick. Flip the flattened dough across the prepared pie plate, using your fingers to press it into the bottom, fix any cracks, and seal around the edges.

¾ cup full-fat coconut milk

½ cup coconut cream (about
   1 [5.4-ounce] can)

1 cup mashed ripe banana
   (about 3 small or
   2 large bananas)

1 ripe avocado

2 Medjool dates, pitted
   (optional), or additional
   1 tablespoon maple syrup

⅓ cup maple syrup

¼ cup unsweetened
   cocoa powder

1 teaspoon vanilla extract

½ teaspoon sea salt

1 tablespoon melted
   coconut oil

Slivered almonds, for
   topping (optional)

6. Bake the crust for 15 to 20 minutes, until slightly golden brown. Set aside and allow the crust to cool completely, at least 1 hour.

7. To make the filling, in a high-speed blender or food processor, mix the coconut milk, coconut cream, banana, avocado, Medjool dates (if using), maple syrup, cocoa powder, vanilla, and salt. Blend until creamy. Add the melted coconut oil and blend again.

8. Pour the mixture into the pie plate with the prebaked crust. Transfer the pie to the refrigerator for 8 to 12 hours to completely set.

Storage: Cover the pie with aluminum foil, and store in the refrigerator for up to 4 days.

Plan-ahead tip: Place a can of coconut cream upside down in the refrigerator the night before (doing so will allow any liquid to remain at the bottom when turned right-side up, leaving the solidified cream at the top). Reserve the liquid for smoothies, or freeze in an ice cube tray for later use.

Ingredient tip: While still in the peel, massage the banana with your hands until very soft. Scrape the contents into a bowl or measuring cup, and mash with a fork until creamy.

Pecan Pie

GRAIN-FREE • PREP AHEAD • SOY-FREE | **Serves:** 8 to 10

Prep time: 30 minutes, plus 30 minutes to chill
Cook time: 50 minutes | **Cooling time:** 4 hours
Equipment: Hand mixer or stand mixer, 9-inch pie plate, rolling pin

Is a holiday dinner complete without pecan pie? It was always served in my household growing up, and I have not skipped a beat by swapping it out with this recipe. The traditional Southern dessert is typically filled with eggs, butter, and sugar, but you can't tell those components are missing in this vegan version. For the record, my family members (who are neither gluten-free nor vegan) have not been able to tell the difference!

FOR THE CRUST

1¾ cups almond flour

¼ cup tapioca flour or arrowroot starch

3 tablespoons coconut sugar

2 teaspoons ground cinnamon

¼ teaspoon sea salt

¼ cup melted coconut oil

¼ cup maple syrup

1 teaspoon vanilla extract

1 teaspoon apple cider vinegar

Nonstick cooking spray

1. To make the crust, in a large bowl or stand mixer, combine the almond flour, tapioca flour, coconut sugar, cinnamon, and salt, using your fingers or the back of a wooden spoon to break up clumps as needed.

2. In a medium bowl, combine the melted coconut oil, maple syrup, vanilla, and vinegar. Whisk until creamy.

3. Pour the wet ingredients into the flour mixture, and beat until a crumbly dough forms. Use your hands to gather the dough into a ball. Wrap the dough tightly in plastic wrap, and refrigerate for 30 minutes.

4. While the dough chills, preheat the oven to 350°F. Spray a 9-inch pie plate with cooking spray.

5. Place the ball of dough between two sheets of parchment paper. Using a rolling pin, roll it out to ⅛ to ¼ inch thick. Flip the flattened dough across the prepared pie plate, using your fingers to press it into the bottom, fix any cracks, and seal around the edges. Place the pie plate in the refrigerator until ready to use.

⅓ cup coconut oil or
    vegan butter

¾ cup maple syrup

½ cup coconut sugar or
    granulated sugar

2 cups roughly
    chopped pecans

½ cup full-fat coconut milk

2 teaspoons vanilla extract

¼ cup arrowroot starch

6. To make the filling, in a small saucepan, combine the coconut oil, maple syrup, and coconut sugar. Heat over medium-low heat and bring to a light simmer. Cook for 1 to 2 more minutes, stirring frequently, watching it carefully to make sure it doesn't burn. Remove from the heat and allow to cool for about 10 minutes (the mixture may become discolored as it cools, but that is normal; just whisk it away).

7. Meanwhile, in another large bowl, place the chopped pecans.

8. Whisk the coconut milk and vanilla into the filling mixture. Pour the mixture over the chopped pecans, and stir until combined. Add the arrowroot starch, and immediately whisk again vigorously until everything fully incorporates. Pour the mixture on top of the crust in the pie plate.

9. Bake for 45 to 50 minutes, until the filling bubbles and a thin crust forms on top (it will feel caramelized and slightly firm to the touch). Allow the pie to cool completely at room temperature, at least 4 hours, before serving.

Storage: Cover loosely with aluminum foil, and store at room temperature for up to 4 days. You can also keep the pie in the refrigerator for up to 1 week, but I recommend allowing the pie to come to room temperature before serving.

Apple-Fig Crumble Pie

GRAIN-FREE • PREP AHEAD • SOY-FREE | Serves: 8 to 10

Prep time: 45 minutes, plus 30 minutes to chill
Cook time: 50 minutes | **Cooling time:** 2 hours
Equipment: Hand mixer or stand mixer, 9-inch pie plate, rolling pin

With a simple tweak to a traditional dessert, this apple pie variation is one of my favorite flavor profiles. The figs offer a unique and natural sweetness, so little additional sugar is needed, and the two fruits complement each other beautifully. I suggest enjoying a serving alongside some vegan vanilla ice cream!

FOR THE CRUST

1¾ cups almond flour

¼ cup tapioca flour or arrowroot starch

3 tablespoons coconut sugar

2 teaspoons ground cinnamon

¼ teaspoon sea salt

¼ cup melted coconut oil

¼ cup maple syrup

1 teaspoon vanilla extract

1 teaspoon apple cider vinegar

Nonstick cooking spray

1. To make the crust, in a large bowl or stand mixer, combine the almond flour, tapioca flour, coconut sugar, cinnamon, and salt, using your fingers or the back of a wooden spoon to break up clumps as needed.

2. In a medium bowl, combine the melted coconut oil, maple syrup, vanilla, and vinegar. Whisk until creamy.

3. Pour the wet ingredients into the flour mixture, and beat until a crumbly dough forms. Use your hands to gather the dough into a ball. Wrap the dough tightly in plastic wrap, and refrigerate for 30 minutes.

4. While the dough chills, preheat the oven to 350°F. Spray a 9-inch pie plate with cooking spray.

5. To start the filling, in a medium bowl, cover the figs with boiling water. Soak for 15 to 20 minutes, until soft. Drain, roughly chop, and set aside.

6. Place the ball of dough between two sheets of parchment paper. Using a rolling pin, roll it out to ⅛ to ¼ inch thick. Flip the flattened dough across the prepared pie plate, using your fingers to press it into the bottom, fix any cracks, and seal around the edges.

FOR THE FILLING

1½ to 2 cups dried whole figs (I suggest white Turkish figs)

¼ cup coconut oil or vegan butter

4 cups diced apples (about 3 apples)

¼ cup coconut sugar

Juice of ½ lemon

1 tablespoon ground cinnamon

1 teaspoon ground nutmeg

1 teaspoon vanilla extract

½ teaspoon ground allspice

⅛ teaspoon ground cloves

⅛ teaspoon sea salt

FOR THE CRUMBLE TOPPING

1 cup almond flour

¼ cup coconut sugar

1 tablespoon coconut flour or additional 1 tablespoon almond flour

1 teaspoon ground cinnamon

⅓ cup cold vegan butter, cut into 1-inch pieces

7. Prebake the crust for 10 minutes, then set aside until ready to use.

8. To finish the filling, in a large pot or Dutch oven, heat the coconut oil over medium-high heat. Add the apples and coconut sugar, and toss to coat. Add the chopped figs, lemon juice, cinnamon, nutmeg, vanilla, allspice, cloves, and salt. Toss to coat. Cook for 15 to 20 minutes, stirring occasionally, until the apples are soft and flavors have melded. Reduce the heat as needed halfway through cooking to maintain a low simmer.

9. Transfer the apple-fig mixture to the prebaked crust.

10. To make the crumble topping, in a medium bowl, combine the almond flour, coconut sugar, coconut flour, and cinnamon. Stir to blend. Add the vegan butter and use your hands to mix and massage it into the flour mixture until a crumble forms. Sprinkle the crumble over the apple-fig mixture.

11. Bake for 20 to 24 minutes, until the crumble has started to turn golden brown. Allow the pie to cool completely, about 2 hours.

Storage: Cover loosely with aluminum foil, and store at room temperature for up to 3 days or in the refrigerator for up to 5 days.

Ingredient tip: If you would like to make this pie with just apples, add another 1 cup diced apple and increase the coconut sugar to ½ cup.

Key Lime Pie

GRAIN-FREE • PREP AHEAD • SOY-FREE | **Serves: 8 to 10**

Prep time: 30 minutes, plus 4 to 6 hours for soaking and 30 minutes to chill
Cook time: 55 minutes | **Cooling time:** 8 hours
Equipment: Box grater, hand mixer or stand mixer, 9-inch
pie plate, rolling pin, high-speed blender

Key lime pie is a popular American dessert. Given that the juice of the key lime is said to be tarter and more aromatic than its conventional cousin, it is traditionally mixed with egg yolks and sweetened condensed milk. In this plant-based pie, lime juice, cashews, coconut cream, and vegan cream cheese come together to create an authentically sweet and citrusy taste. I have used both key limes and regular limes in the past for this recipe, and both work well.

FOR THE CRUST

1¾ cups almond flour

¼ cup tapioca flour or
   arrowroot starch

3 tablespoons coconut sugar

¼ teaspoon sea salt

¼ cup melted coconut oil

¼ cup maple syrup

1 teaspoon vanilla extract

1 teaspoon apple cider vinegar

Nonstick cooking spray

1. To make the crust, in a large bowl or stand mixer, combine the almond flour, tapioca flour, coconut sugar, and salt, using your fingers or the back of a wooden spoon to break up clumps as needed.

2. In a medium bowl, combine the melted coconut oil, maple syrup, vanilla, and vinegar. Whisk until creamy.

3. Pour the wet ingredients into the flour mixture, and beat until a crumbly dough forms. Use your hands to gather the dough into a ball. Wrap the dough tightly in plastic wrap, and refrigerate for 30 minutes.

4. While the dough chills, preheat the oven to 350°F. Spray a 9-inch pie plate with cooking spray.

5. Place the ball of dough between two sheets of parchment paper. Using a rolling pin, roll it out to ⅛ to ¼ inch thick. Flip the flattened dough across the prepared pie plate, using your fingers to press it into the bottom, fix any cracks, and seal around the edges. Place the pie plate in the refrigerator until ready to use.

¾ cup full-fat coconut milk

½ cup maple syrup

½ cup freshly squeezed lime juice (from about 3 large or 4 to 5 small limes)

1 cup raw whole cashews, soaked in water for at least 4 to 6 hours (or, ideally, overnight), drained and rinsed

1 cup coconut cream (about 2 [5.4-ounce] cans)

½ cup vegan cream cheese, at room temperature (I suggest Kite Hill brand)

2 tablespoons arrowroot starch

1 tablespoon grated lime zest (from about 2 limes)

6. To make the filling, in a high-speed blender, combine the coconut milk, maple syrup, lime juice, soaked cashews, coconut cream, vegan cream cheese, arrowroot starch, and lime zest. Blend until creamy.

7. Pour the filling into the pie plate with the crust. Bake for 50 to 55 minutes, until the crust edges are golden brown and the pie edges have started to crust. (The middle should still "jiggle" and may look a bit darker and undercooked, but it will set as it cools. An inserted toothpick should come out clean.) Allow the pie to completely cool at room temperature, about 2 hours, before transferring to the refrigerator for 4 to 6 hours (or, ideally, overnight) to completely set.

Storage: Cover the pie with aluminum foil, and store in the refrigerator for up to 4 days.

Plan-ahead tip: The night before, soak the cashews and place the cans of coconut cream upside down in the refrigerator (doing so will allow any liquid to remain at the bottom when turned right-side up, leaving the solidified cream at the top). Reserve the liquid for smoothies, or freeze in an ice cube tray for later use.

Prep tip: When combining the filling ingredients in a high-speed blender, add the liquid ingredients first. This will make for smoother processing.

Serving tip: Allow the pie to sit out at room temperature for 20 to 30 minutes before serving.

Southern-Style Sweet Potato Pie

GRAIN-FREE • PREP AHEAD • SOY-FREE | Serves: 8 to 10

Prep time: 40 minutes, plus 30 minutes to chill
Cook time: 1 hour 20 minutes minutes | **Cooling time:** 8 hours
Equipment: Hand mixer or stand mixer, baking sheet, 9-inch pie plate,
rolling pin, high-speed blender or food processor (optional)

There is nothing more Southern sounding than a sweet potato pie. Sweet potatoes are one of my favorite foods, and I love the warmth and flavor that the spices contribute to this traditional Southern dessert. I find that it's even better the next day if you want to prepare it in advance. Enjoy with a dollop of coconut whipped cream (see Mississippi Mud Pie with Coconut Whipped Cream, page 154).

FOR THE CRUST

1¾ cups almond flour

¼ cup tapioca flour or arrowroot starch

3 tablespoons coconut sugar

2 teaspoons ground cinnamon

¼ teaspoon sea salt

¼ cup melted coconut oil

¼ cup maple syrup

1 teaspoon vanilla extract

1 teaspoon apple cider vinegar

Nonstick cooking spray

1. To make the crust, in a large bowl or stand mixer, mix the almond flour, tapioca flour, coconut sugar, cinnamon, and salt, using your fingers or the back of a wooden spoon to break up clumps as needed.

2. In a medium bowl, mix the melted coconut oil, maple syrup, vanilla, and vinegar. Whisk until creamy.

3. Pour the wet ingredients into the flour mixture, and beat until a crumbly dough forms. Use your hands to gather the dough into a ball. Wrap the dough tightly in plastic wrap and refrigerate for 30 minutes.

4. Preheat the oven to 400°F. Line a baking sheet with parchment paper.

5. Arrange the sweet potatoes on the prepared baking sheet and toss with the coconut oil. Bake for 30 minutes, until fork-tender. Let cool for 5 to 10 minutes on the baking sheet, then set aside.

6. Reduce the oven temperature for 350°F. Spray a 9-inch pie plate with cooking spray.

4 cups peeled and chopped sweet potatoes (about 2 large or 3 medium sweet potatoes)

1 tablespoon melted coconut oil

¾ cup full-fat coconut milk

2 tablespoons maple syrup

1 teaspoon vanilla extract

¼ cup coconut sugar

2 tablespoons arrowroot starch

2 teaspoons ground cinnamon

1 teaspoon baking powder

½ teaspoon baking soda

½ teaspoon ground nutmeg

¼ teaspoon ground allspice

¼ teaspoon sea salt

⅛ teaspoon ground cloves

7. Place the ball of dough between two sheets of parchment paper. Using a rolling pin, roll it out to ⅛ to ¼ inch thick. Flip the flattened dough across the prepared pie plate, using your fingers to press it into the bottom, fix any cracks, and seal around the edges. Set aside until ready for use.

8. To make the filling, in a high-speed blender or food processor, combine the coconut milk, maple syrup, and vanilla. Add the roasted sweet potatoes along with the coconut sugar, arrowroot starch, cinnamon, baking powder, baking soda, nutmeg, allspice, salt, and cloves. Blend until creamy. If you don't have a food processor or high-speed blender, you can use an immersion blender, hand mixer, or potato masher to beat the sweet potatoes, then whisk the remaining ingredients in by hand.

9. Transfer the sweet potato mixture into the pie crust. Bake for 45 to 50 minutes, until the edges are golden brown and the filling looks set. Allow the pie to completely cool, about 2 hours, before transferring to the refrigerator for at least 4 to 6 hours (or, ideally, overnight) to completely set.

Storage: Cover lightly with aluminum foil, and store in the refrigerator for up to 4 days. Serve chilled or bring to room temperature before serving.

Plan-ahead tip: You can bake the sweet potatoes up to 2 days in advance.

Ingredient tip: For easier preparation, you can buy a box of chopped sweet potatoes or use one (15-ounce) can of sweet potato purée.

Prep tip: When combining the filling ingredients in a high-speed blender or food processor, add the liquid ingredients first. This will make for smoother processing.

Chocolate Fudge Tart

GRAIN-FREE • PREP AHEAD • SOY-FREE | **Serves:** 8

Prep time: 20 minutes, plus 30 minutes to chill
Cook time: 50 minutes | **Cooling time:** 8 hours
Equipment: Hand mixer or stand mixer, 9-inch tart pan, rolling
pin, high-speed blender or food processor (optional)

A thin, crispy crust sits beneath the rich, fudgy filling in this decadent dessert. If you have yet to try making a tart, this recipe is a delicious place to start. A close cousin to pies, tarts are baked in a special pan with a removable bottom (making them very easy to serve), can be sweet or savory, and tend to have a satisfyingly dense texture. The taste and texture are two main things I love about this particular tart, and it is one of my favorite baked goods to make and share with family and friends.

FOR THE CRUST

1½ cups almond flour

3 tablespoons tapioca flour or arrowroot starch

3 tablespoons coconut sugar

¼ teaspoon sea salt

¼ cup maple syrup

3 tablespoons melted coconut oil

1 teaspoon vanilla extract

Nonstick cooking spray

1. To make the crust, in a large bowl or stand mixer, mix the almond flour, tapioca flour, coconut sugar, and salt. Stir to blend.

2. In a medium bowl, mix the maple syrup, melted coconut oil, and vanilla. Whisk.

3. Pour the wet ingredients into the flour mixture, and beat until a dough forms. Gather the dough into a ball. Wrap tightly in plastic wrap and refrigerate for 30 minutes.

4. Preheat the oven to 350°F. Liberally spray a 9-inch tart pan with a removable bottom with cooking spray.

5. Place the ball of dough between two sheets of parchment paper. Using a rolling pin, roll the dough until about ¼ inch thick. Flip it onto the prepared tart pan, and carefully press it into the bottom, discarding any excess dough. Place the pan in the refrigerator until ready to use.

6. To make the filling, in a small saucepan over medium heat, combine the chocolate chips and coconut oil. Heat until melted, 2 to 3 minutes, stirring frequently (be careful not to let it burn). Remove from the heat and set aside.

**1 cup dairy-free
chocolate chips**

**¼ cup coconut oil,
softened or melted**

1 cup full-fat coconut milk

1 cup pumpkin purée

¾ cup coconut sugar

**½ cup unsweetened
cocoa powder**

¼ cup arrowroot starch

⅓ cup maple syrup

½ teaspoon baking powder

1 teaspoon vanilla extract

¼ teaspoon sea salt

7. In a high-speed blender or food processor, mix the coconut milk, pumpkin purée, coconut sugar, cocoa powder, arrowroot starch, maple syrup, baking powder, vanilla, and salt. Blend until creamy. You can also whisk everything together by hand in a medium bowl. Add the melted chocolate mixture and blend again. Pour the mixture into the tart pan with the crust.

8. Bake for 45 to 50 minutes, until the crust edges are golden brown and the filling forms a thin crust. (The filling may look like it has risen too high, but it will come down and set as it cools.) Allow the tart to completely cool in the pan, about 2 hours, before transferring to the refrigerator for at least 4 to 6 hours (or, ideally, overnight) to completely set.

Storage: Wrap the whole tart or individual slices in aluminum foil or plastic wrap, and store in the refrigerator for up to 5 days.

Peanut Butter and Jelly Tart

GRAIN-FREE • PREP AHEAD • SOY-FREE | Serves: 8 to 10

Prep time: 45 minutes, plus 30 minutes to chill
Cook time: 50 minutes | **Cooling time:** 8 hours
Equipment: Hand mixer or stand mixer, 9-inch tart pan,
rolling pin, high-speed blender or food processor

Who said peanut butter and jelly is only for kids? I call this an adult-sized version of the adored childhood classic. However, that doesn't exclude kids from enjoying this dish as well! I believe anyone at any age will love it. For the jam topping, use the blackberry-chia jam recipe provided or 1 cup of any store-bought jelly or jam of choice.

FOR THE CRUST

1½ cups almond flour

3 tablespoons tapioca flour
   or arrowroot starch

3 tablespoons coconut sugar

¼ teaspoon sea salt

¼ cup maple syrup

3 tablespoons melted
   coconut oil

1 teaspoon vanilla extract

Nonstick cooking spray

1. To make the crust, in a large bowl or stand mixer, mix the almond flour, tapioca flour, coconut sugar, and salt. Stir to blend.

2. In a medium bowl, mix the maple syrup, melted coconut oil, and vanilla. Whisk until creamy.

3. Pour the wet ingredients into the flour mixture, and beat until a dough forms. Gather the dough into a ball. Wrap tightly in plastic wrap and refrigerate for 30 minutes.

4. Preheat the oven to 350°F. Liberally spray a 9-inch tart pan with a removable bottom with cooking spray.

5. Place the ball of dough between two sheets of parchment paper. Using a rolling pin, roll the dough until about ¼ inch thick. Flip it onto the prepared tart pan, and carefully press it into the bottom, discarding any excess dough. Place the pan in the refrigerator until ready to use.

6. To make the filling, in a high-speed blender or food processor, combine the coconut milk, coconut cream, peanut butter, vegan cream cheese, coconut sugar, arrowroot starch, maple syrup, vanilla, baking powder, and salt. Blend until creamy.

½ cup full-fat coconut milk

1 cup coconut cream (about
2 [5.4-ounce] cans)

¾ cup creamy peanut butter

½ cup vegan cream cheese,
at room temperature

½ cup coconut sugar

2 tablespoons
arrowroot starch

2 tablespoons maple syrup

1 teaspoon vanilla extract

½ teaspoon baking powder

¼ teaspoon sea salt

2 cups frozen blackberries

Juice of ½ lemon

¼ cup maple syrup

2 tablespoons chia seeds

7. Pour the filling into the tart pan with the crust. Bake for 45 to 50 minutes, until the edges of the crust are golden brown and the top forms a thin crust. (The filling may look like it has risen too high, but it will come down and set as it cools.) Allow to completely cool in the tart pan at room temperature, at least 2 hours.

8. To make the blackberry-chia jam, in a medium saucepan over medium-high heat, combine the blackberries, lemon juice, and maple syrup. Cover and bring to a boil for about 5 minutes. Remove the lid and stir, breaking up the berries with the back of a wooden spoon. Reduce the heat to a medium low and simmer until the liquid has reduced by half, 10 to 15 minutes.

9. Transfer the mixture to a small bowl, and add the chia seeds. For the first 5 to 10 minutes, stir frequently with a fork to prevent the chia seeds from clumping. Set aside to allow the mixture to gel and cool, about 1 hour. Once the tart and jam have cooled, carefully spread the jam on top of the tart. Transfer the tart to the refrigerator for at least 4 to 6 hours (or, ideally, overnight) to completely set.

Storage: Wrap the whole tart or individual slices in aluminum foil or plastic wrap, and store in the refrigerator for up to 5 days.

Prep tip: If you don't have a 9-inch tart pan, you can use a 9-inch pie plate instead, but the crust may turn out a bit thinner.

Plan-ahead tip: The jam can be made up to 4 to 5 days in advance. Keep it in an airtight container or mason jar in the refrigerator until ready to use.

Vegan Custard Mini Tarts

GRAIN-FREE • PREP AHEAD • SOY-FREE | **Makes:** 6 tarts

Prep time: 20 minutes, plus 30 minutes to chill
Cook time: 25 minutes | **Cooling time:** 9 hours
Equipment: Hand mixer or stand mixer, six 4-inch tart
pans, rolling pin, high-speed blender (optional)

When I concocted a vegan custard, I immediately imagined it in a
tart of some sort. Surrounded by a cakey crust, the sugary custard
filling is the star here. These individual desserts are so fun to serve
to a small group, and they are as delicious as they are cute.

FOR THE CRUST

1½ cups almond flour

3 tablespoons tapioca flour
or arrowroot starch

3 tablespoons coconut sugar

¼ teaspoon sea salt

¼ cup maple syrup

3 tablespoons melted
coconut oil

1 teaspoon vanilla extract

Nonstick cooking spray

FOR THE CUSTARD

1 (13.5-ounce) can full-
fat coconut milk

2 teaspoons vanilla extract

½ cup maple syrup

¼ cup arrowroot starch

1. To make the crust, in a large bowl or stand mixer, mix the almond flour, tapioca flour, coconut sugar, and salt. Stir to blend.

2. In a medium bowl, mix the maple syrup, melted coconut oil, and vanilla. Whisk until creamy.

3. Pour the wet ingredients into the flour mixture. Beat until a dough forms. Gather the dough into a ball. Wrap tightly in plastic wrap and refrigerate for 30 minutes.

4. While the dough chills, preheat the oven to 350°F. Spray six 4-inch tart pans with removable bottoms with cooking spray.

5. Using a rolling pin, roll the dough between two sheets of parchment paper until about ¼ inch thick. Using a knife, cut 6 circles, each about 5 inches in diameter. Use a spatula sprayed with cooking spray to carefully place the dough rounds over the prepared mini tart pans, and use your fingers to press each into the bottom and seal around the edges, using any excess dough to fill any cracks.

6. Bake for 15 minutes, until golden brown. Set aside until ready to use.

7. To make the custard, in a medium saucepan, combine the coconut milk and vanilla. Bring to a boil over high heat. Add the maple syrup and arrowroot starch, and whisk. If you have a high-speed blender, transfer the mixture to the blender and process until smooth (otherwise, whisk vigorously by hand, breaking up any clumps). Place the mixture back in the saucepan, reduce the heat to medium low and simmer for 7 to 10 minutes, until it thickens, stirring occasionally. The custard is ready when you stir with a spatula and it creates "ribbons."

8. Divide the custard evenly among the mini tart pans (there might be a little bit of custard left over). Allow the custard to cool completely in the tart pans at room temperature, about 1 hour, before transferring to the refrigerator for 8 hours or, ideally, up to 24 hours to completely set.

Storage: Wrap individual tarts in plastic wrap or aluminum foil, and store in the refrigerator for up to 4 days.

Serving tip: Right before serving, dollop with coconut whipped cream (see Mississippi Mud Pie with Coconut Whipped Cream, page 154) and place a few berries on top.

Coconut Cream Pie

GRAIN-FREE • PREP AHEAD • SOY-FREE | Serves: 8 to 10

Prep time: 30 minutes, plus 3 hours to chill
Cook time: 25 minutes | **Cooling time:** 15 hours
Equipment: Hand mixer or stand mixer, 9-inch pie plate,
rolling pin, high-speed blender (optional)

If you're a coconut fan, you're going to love this pie! The coconut whipped cream appropriately acts as one of the main ingredients in this dessert, but combined with nutty, crunchy shredded coconut, this pie's consistency offers the best of both worlds. You can even toast the shredded coconut to enhance the flavor even further.

FOR THE CRUST

1¾ cups almond flour

¼ cup tapioca flour or arrowroot starch

3 tablespoons coconut sugar

¼ teaspoon sea salt

¼ cup melted coconut oil

¼ cup maple syrup

1 teaspoon vanilla extract

1 teaspoon apple cider vinegar

Nonstick cooking spray

1. To make the crust, in a large bowl or stand mixer, mix the almond flour, tapioca flour, coconut sugar, and salt, using your fingers or the back of a wooden spoon to break up clumps as needed.

2. In a medium bowl, combine the melted coconut oil, maple syrup, vanilla, and vinegar. Whisk until creamy.

3. Pour the wet ingredients into the flour mixture, and beat until a crumbly dough forms. Use your hands to gather the dough into a ball. Wrap the dough tightly in plastic wrap and refrigerate for 30 minutes.

4. While the dough chills, preheat the oven to 350°F. Spray a 9-inch pie plate with cooking spray.

5. Place the ball of dough between two sheets of parchment paper. Using a rolling pin, roll it out to ⅛ to ¼ inch thick. Flip the flattened dough across the prepared pie plate, using your fingers to press it into the bottom, fix any cracks, and seal around the edges.

6. Bake for 20 to 25 minutes, until golden brown. Set aside to cool until ready to use.

FOR THE FILLING

1 (13.5-ounce) can full-
fat coconut milk

3 teaspoons vanilla
extract, divided

½ cup maple syrup,
plus 2 tablespoons

¼ cup arrowroot starch

2 cups coconut cream (about
4 [5.4-ounce] cans)

½ cup unsweetened
shredded coconut, plus
more for topping, if desired

7. To make the filling, in a medium saucepan, combine the coconut milk and 2 tablespoons of vanilla. Bring to a boil. Add ½ cup of maple syrup, and whisk vigorously until combined.

8. If you have a high-speed blender, transfer the mixture to the blender and add the arrowroot starch. Process until smooth (otherwise, add the arrowroot starch along with the ½ cup of maple syrup to the saucepan, and whisk vigorously by hand, breaking up any clumps). Place the mixture back in the saucepan, reduce the heat to medium low and simmer for 10 minutes, until it thickens, stirring occasionally. The mixture is ready when you stir with a spatula and it creates ribbons.

9. Transfer the filling mixture to a small glass bowl. Allow the filling to come to room temperature, at least 1 hour, then place a piece of plastic wrap over the bowl and touching the filling to prevent a film from forming on top. Place in the refrigerator to chill for 2 hours.

10. Once chilled, place a medium bowl in the freezer for 5 to 10 minutes. Spoon the coconut cream into the chilled bowl, draining any coconut water. Use a hand mixer to beat the coconut cream on high speed until fluffy, about 1 minute. Add the remaining 2 tablespoons of maple syrup and remaining 1 teaspoon of vanilla. Beat again for 30 seconds. Reserve 1 cup of the whipped cream and set aside.

11. Fold the chilled filling into the bowl of coconut whipped cream. Add the shredded coconut and fold again.

12. Transfer the cream mixture to the baked pie crust. Use a spatula to spread the reserved cup of coconut whipped cream on top, and sprinkle some more shredded coconut over it, if desired. Transfer to the refrigerator for 8 to 12 hours, or up to 24 hours, to completely set.

Storage: Cover the pie with aluminum foil, and store in the refrigerator for up to 4 days.

Mississippi Mud Pie with Coconut Whipped Cream

GRAIN-FREE • PREP AHEAD • SOY-FREE | **Serves:** 8 to 10

Prep time: 40 minutes, plus 30 minutes to chill
Cook time: 50 minutes | **Cooling time:** 10 hours
Equipment: Hand mixer or stand mixer, 9-inch pie plate, rolling
pin, high-speed blender or food processor (optional)

This dessert's unique design contributes to its descriptive moniker. It is said to have originated in the state it is named after, with its rich, chocolaty layers looking like the bottom of the Mississippi River. The chocolate crust is filled with a creamy chocolate mixture, then finished with a coconut whipped cream topping. A slice is traditionally served with ice cream, so scoop your favorite vegan version right alongside to complete the treat!

FOR THE CRUST

1¾ cups almond flour

3 tablespoons tapioca flour
or arrowroot starch

3 tablespoons coconut sugar

2 tablespoons unsweetened
cocoa powder

¼ teaspoon sea salt

¼ cup melted coconut oil

¼ cup maple syrup

1 teaspoon vanilla extract

Nonstick cooking spray

1. To make the crust, in a large bowl or stand mixer, mix the almond flour, tapioca flour, coconut sugar, cocoa powder, and salt. Stir to blend.

2. In a medium bowl, mix the melted coconut oil, maple syrup, and vanilla. Whisk until creamy.

3. Pour the wet ingredients into the flour mixture, and beat until a dough forms. Gather the dough into a ball. Wrap tightly in plastic wrap and refrigerate for 30 minutes.

4. While the dough chills, preheat the oven to 350°F. Spray a 9-inch pie plate with cooking spray.

5. Place the ball of the dough between two sheets of parchment paper. Using a rolling pin, roll the dough until about ¼ inch thick. Flip the crust onto the prepared pie plate, and use your fingers to press it into the bottom of the plate and seal where needed. Place the pie plate in the refrigerator until ready to use.

1 cup dairy-free
  chocolate chips

¼ cup coconut oil,
  softened or melted

1 cup full-fat coconut milk

⅓ cup maple syrup

1 cup pumpkin purée

¾ cup coconut sugar

½ cup unsweetened
  cocoa powder

¼ cup arrowroot starch

1 teaspoon vanilla extract

¼ teaspoon sea salt

FOR THE COCONUT
WHIPPED CREAM

1 cup coconut cream (about
  2 [5.4-ounce] cans)

1 tablespoon maple syrup

½ teaspoon vanilla extract

6. To make the filling, in a small saucepan over medium heat, mix the chocolate chips and coconut oil. Heat until melted, 2 to 3 minutes, stirring frequently (be careful not to let it burn). Remove from the heat and set aside.

7. In a high-speed blender or food processor, mix the coconut milk, maple syrup, pumpkin purée, coconut sugar, cocoa powder, arrowroot starch, vanilla, and salt. Blend until creamy. You can also whisk everything together by hand in a medium bowl. Add the melted chocolate mixture and blend again. Pour the mixture into the prepared crust.

8. Bake for 45 to 50 minutes, until the edges are firm to the touch and have started to crust. (The center of the pie will appear darker and look underdone, but it will set as it cools.) Allow the pie to completely cool at room temperature, about 2 hours, before transferring to the refrigerator for at least 6 to 8 hours or, ideally, overnight.

9. To make the coconut whipped cream, place a medium bowl in the freezer for 5 to 10 minutes. Spoon the coconut cream into the bowl, draining any coconut water. Use a hand mixer to beat the coconut cream on high speed until fluffy, about 1 minute. Add the maple syrup and vanilla extract. Beat again for 30 seconds. Spread the whipped cream on top of the chilled pie.

Storage: Cover the pie with aluminum foil, and store in the refrigerator for up to 3 days.

Serving tip: I recommend topping the pie with the coconut whipped cream on the same day you are ready to serve. Serve immediately, or place the pie in the refrigerator for 30 minutes to allow the whipped cream topping to chill.

Savory Butternut Squash Tart

GRAIN-FREE • PREP AHEAD • SOY-FREE | Serves: 8 to 10

Prep time: 1 hour, plus 30 minutes to chill
Cook time: 50 minutes | **Cooling time:** 4 hours
Equipment: Hand mixer or stand mixer, 9-inch tart pan, rolling pin, food processor

The tart's filling was inspired by one of my favorite dinner side dishes that I call "the best butternut mash," and with only a few alterations, it became this oh-so-flavorful baked good. It is amazing what some spices can do. The chickpea miso adds to its unique flavor profile, but feel free to use the substitutions below. Either way, this dish makes a great meal for any part of the day.

FOR THE CRUST

1½ cups almond flour

¼ cup nutritional yeast

½ teaspoon sea salt

3 tablespoons full-fat coconut milk or unsweetened almond milk

¼ cup melted coconut oil

Nonstick cooking spray

1. To make the crust, in a large bowl or stand mixer, mix the almond flour, nutritional yeast, and salt. Stir to blend.

2. While beating on medium speed, add the coconut milk. Continue to beat, and slowly incorporate the melted coconut oil, increasing the speed as needed, until a dough forms. Gather the dough into a ball. Wrap tightly in plastic wrap and refrigerate for 30 minutes.

3. Preheat the oven to 350°F. Spray a 9-inch tart pan with a removable bottom with cooking spray.

4. Place the ball of dough between two sheets of parchment paper. Using a rolling pin, roll the dough until about ¼ inch thick. Flip it onto the prepared tart pan, and carefully press it into the bottom, discarding any excess dough. Place the pan in the refrigerator until ready to use.

5. To make the filling, in a food processor, combine the roasted butternut squash, coconut milk, nutritional yeast, miso, arrowroot starch, vegan butter, lemon juice, mustard, garlic powder, onion powder, salt, and pepper. Blend until creamy, scraping down the sides as needed. Using a spatula, transfer the filling to the tart pan and evenly distribute.

2 to 2½ cups roasted cubed
butternut squash

½ cup full-fat coconut milk or
unsweetened almond milk

3 tablespoons
nutritional yeast

2 tablespoons chickpea miso

2 tablespoons
arrowroot starch

1 tablespoon vegan butter

Juice of ½ lemon

2 teaspoons Dijon or
spicy brown mustard

½ teaspoon garlic powder

½ teaspoon onion powder

½ teaspoon sea salt

Pinch freshly ground
black pepper

6. Bake for 45 to 50 minutes, until the top forms a thin crust and started to turn golden brown. The center should still feel soft. Allow the tart to cool for 4 hours in the pan at room temperature before serving.

Storage: Wrap individual slices tightly in plastic wrap, and store in the refrigerator for up to 4 days. Reheat before serving.

Ingredient tip: Four cups of raw cubed butternut squash yields 2 to 2½ cups when roasted. Buy a box of prechopped butternut squash for easy preparation, or use butternut squash purée from a can. You can also use frozen butternut squash; just follow the thawing and roasting instructions on the package. Chickpea miso is made from fermented chickpeas, and I suggest either the South River or Miso Master brand. You can substitute it with white miso (made from fermented soybeans, so the result wouldn't be soy-free) or tahini instead.

Plan-ahead tip: While the dough chills in the refrigerator, roast the butternut squash in a 400°F oven for 25 to 30 minutes, until fork-tender. You can also roast the squash a day in advance and refrigerate until ready to use.

Measurement Conversions

VOLUME EQUIVALENTS (LIQUID)

US STANDARD	US STANDARD (OUNCES)	METRIC (APPROXIMATE)
2 tablespoons	1 fl. oz.	30 mL
¼ cup	2 fl. oz.	60 mL
½ cup	4 fl. oz.	120 mL
1 cup	8 fl. oz.	240 mL
1½ cups	12 fl. oz.	355 mL
2 cups or 1 pint	16 fl. oz.	475 mL
4 cups or 1 quart	32 fl. oz.	1 L
1 gallon	128 fl. oz.	4 L

OVEN TEMPERATURES

FAHRENHEIT (F)	CELSIUS (C) (APPROXIMATE)
250°F	120°C
300°F	150°C
325°F	165°C
350°F	180°C
375°F	190°C
400°F	200°C
425°F	220°C
450°F	230°C

VOLUME EQUIVALENTS (DRY)

US STANDARD	METRIC (APPROXIMATE)
⅛ teaspoon	0.5 mL
¼ teaspoon	1 mL
½ teaspoon	2 mL
¾ teaspoon	4 mL
1 teaspoon	5 mL
1 tablespoon	15 mL
¼ cup	59 mL
⅓ cup	79 mL
½ cup	118 mL
⅔ cup	156 mL
¾ cup	177 mL
1 cup	235 mL
2 cups or 1 pint	475 mL
3 cups	700 mL
4 cups or 1 quart	1 L

WEIGHT EQUIVALENTS

US STANDARD	METRIC (APPROXIMATE)
½ ounce	15 g
1 ounce	30 g
2 ounces	60 g
4 ounces	115 g
8 ounces	225 g
12 ounces	340 g
16 ounces or 1 pound	455 g

Weights of Common Baking Ingredients

	VOLUME	GRAMS	OUNCES
Almond flour	1 cup	96	3.375
All-purpose gluten-free flour	1 cup	136	4.8
Arrowroot starch	¼ cup	32	1.13
Cocoa powder	2 tablespoons	11	0.375
Coconut flour	¼ cup	32	1.13
Coconut palm sugar	½ cup	100	3.5
Golden flaxseed meal	2 tablespoons	13	1
Oat flour	¼ cup	30	1.05
Rice flour (brown)	1 cup	160	5.7
Rice flour (white)	1 cup	160	5.7
Sugar (granulated cane)	½ cup	126	4.41
Tapioca flour	¼ cup	30	1.07

Pan Size Substitutions

IF YOU DON'T HAVE	YOU CAN USE
2 Round 8" Pans	1—12-cup capacity Bundt pan
	2—9" pans
	1—10" round or square pan
	24 muffins or cupcakes
	1—12" x 18" x 1" sheet pan
	1—9" x 13" x 2" rectangle pan
	2—8" square pans
	1—10" round springform pan
1 Round 7" pan	1—8" pan
Standard Loaf 9" x 5" x 3"	1—8" round or square pan
	1—9" round or square pan
	1—6-cup capacity Bundt pan
	12 cupcakes or muffins
1 — 8" Deep Dish Pie Plate (8" x 2")	1—8" round cake pan
	1—8" tart pan
1—8" Square Casserole Dish	1—8" square pan
1—9" x 13" Casserole	1—10" pie plate
	1—9" x 13" cake pan
Standard 12-Muffin Tin 2¾" Wide x 1¼" Deep	1—8" cake pan
	1 standard loaf pan

Substitutions

GLUTEN-FREE VEGAN BAKING SUBSTITUTES FOR CONVENTIONAL RECIPES

Many of the ingredients found in conventional baking are not included in a gluten-free and vegan diet. Fortunately, with the help of certain substitutes, plant-based replacements, and various products that have come on the market, baking can be enjoyed by everyone, even those with these dietary restrictions. I have included a table here listing some of the main items that are used in traditional baking, the purpose they serve, and what you can use instead to fit your needs. Hopefully you find this information useful, whether you are baking from this book or otherwise.

I also understand that some of the ingredients listed in these recipes might not be available to you. I have included a second table listing gluten-free and vegan substitutions for items in this book, with the ratio or amount needed. For best results, the recipes should be followed as written, so know that taste, texture, and cook time may vary depending on any changes that you make.

SUBSTIUTIONS FOR COMMON INGREDIENTS

INGREDIENT	PURPOSE	SUBSTITUTES
Butter	Provides a creamy, fatty mouthfeel and taste. A binding agent that also contributes to texture and helps with rising.	Vegan butter, unrefined coconut oil, olive oil, mashed avocado, mashed banana, applesauce, palm oil shortening
Buttermilk	Slightly acidic, buttermilk assists with the chemical breakdown of other ingredients, leading to a moist result. It also adds a tangy flavor to baked goods.	Lemon juice or vinegar added to dairy-free milk of choice (for every 1 cup milk, whisk in 1 tablespoon freshly squeezed lemon juice or 1 teaspoon apple cider vinegar or white vinegar)

INGREDIENT	PURPOSE	SUBSTITUTES
Chocolate	Provides flavor.	Dairy-free chocolate chips or chocolate bars (such as Enjoy Life brand), unsweetened cocoa powder, raw cacao powder
Cream	With more fat content than milk, cream is more about acting as a binding or thickening agent than just adding moisture. It also provides a creamy taste and texture.	Full-fat coconut cream, cashew cream, dairy-free yogurt, vegan butter
Cream cheese	A slightly acidic fat source that adds a unique texture and taste. It can mostly be found in frostings and as a base in cheesecakes.	Vegan cream cheese (such as Kite Hill and Go Veggie brands)
Eggs	Eggs are primarily a binding agent that helps with rising. Egg yolks provide a creamy taste and texture. Egg whites provide moisture and a fluffy result.	Flax eggs, chia eggs, egg substitutes (such as Bob's Red Mill brand), aquafaba (from the water found in a can of chickpeas), mashed banana, dairy-free yogurt
Flour	A common ingredient that holds other ingredients together. Provides structure for batter or dough.	Gluten-free flour, grain-free flour, starch
Honey	A thick, viscous liquid sweetener. Also provides moisture.	Maple syrup, coconut nectar, brown rice syrup, agave nectar
Milk	Chemically, milk is composed of protein, sugar, and fat, which all serve a purpose. It lends structure, taste, and texture to batter or dough and also provides moisture.	Full-fat coconut milk, almond milk, cashew milk, macadamia nut milk, soy milk
Yogurt	Provides a spongy texture to baked goods. Also a source of fat, and its acidity can assist with rising.	Dairy-free yogurt, cashew cream, coconut cream

SUBSTITUTIONS FOR INGREDIENTS IN THIS BOOK

INGREDIENT	SUBSTITUTES	AMOUNT
Almond flour	Cashew flour, hazelnut flour, sunflower meal	Substitute 1:1.
Arrowroot starch	Cornstarch or tapioca flour	Use ½ tablespoon cornstarch for every 1 tablespoon arrowroot starch. Substitute tapioca flour 1:1.
Coconut sugar	White sugar, brown sugar, raw or turbinado sugar	Substitute granulated sugar of choice 1:1.
Coconut milk	Almond milk or any other dairy-free milk of choice	Substitute 1:1.
Coconut oil	Melted vegan butter, olive oil, safflower oil	Substitute 1:1.
Maple syrup	Liquid sweetener of choice	Substitute 1:1.
Gluten-free all-purpose flour	Homemade gluten-free flour blend	Use 1½ cups brown rice flour + ½ cup potato starch + ¼ cup white rice flour + ¼ cup tapioca flour, or use 2 cups almond flour + 1½ cups arrowroot starch + 1½ cups coconut flour + 1 cup tapioca flour.
Tapioca flour	Cornstarch or arrowroot starch	Use ½ tablespoon cornstarch for every 1 tablespoon tapioca flour. Substitute arrowroot starch 1:1.
Vegan butter	Unrefined coconut oil or nondairy margarine	Substitute 1:1.

Resources

BOB'S RED MILL. When it comes to gluten-free and grain-free flours, Bob's Red Mill is my favorite and most trusted brand. The company sells all of the flours included in the recipes in this book: nut flours, rice flours, oat flour, coconut flour, and starches. www.bobsredmill.com

THRIVE MARKET. A subscription-based online retailer for natural and organic food at a reduced cost. Thrive Market is an amazing platform and an easy-to-navigate website for finding gluten-free and vegan ingredients, featuring many of my favorite brands at a lower price than you might find in the grocery store. www.thrivemarket.com

IHERB. Another online retailer that prides itself on providing natural and organic products at a lower price (almost like Amazon for natural food, and no subscription is needed). It is another great option for pantry staples with trusted brands, such as Bob's Red Mill, Nutiva, and Artisana. www.iherb.com

WHOLE FOODS AND TRADER JOE'S. Whole Foods is my favorite brick-and-mortar, one-stop shop for baking supplies. The store has a great bulk bin section as well. While Trader Joe's is on a smaller scale, prices tend to be lower, and it is a great place to buy nuts, nut butters, oils, canned goods, and other baking staples to stock your pantry. www.wholefoodsmarket.com, www.traderjoes.com

MINIMALIST BAKER. Dana Schultz is the food blogger behind MinimalistBaker. com, a website filled with plant-based recipes that are primarily gluten-free. Her recipes are easy to make, and she is great about offering her readers substitutions and tips. www.minimalistbaker.com

PINTEREST. With the plethora of food bloggers on the Internet, there is an abundance of recipes at your fingertips. I use Pinterest on a weekly basis for recipe inspiration. I suggest typing the keywords "gluten-free vegan baking" in the search bar or specifying the type of gluten-free vegan baked good you are looking for. www.pinterest.com

Recipe Index

Index

Acknowledgments

There are so many people I am grateful for, both for their contribution to this cookbook and in general.

Alex, thank you for being my best friend and biggest fan. Your partnership and support give me the confidence to achieve my dreams. Most importantly, thank you for eating cake for breakfast with me throughout the process of this project and for cleaning the kitchen when I was too tapped out to do so.

Mom, thank you for being my first baking partner. You are the reason why I love creating in the kitchen. Dad, there is no way I would be where I am in my work without you. To make you proud has been my number one driving force to go after my dreams. I miss you every day.

Laura Lea, I am forever grateful for our friendship. You have shown me what is possible. Thank you for your encouragement to stay aligned with my authentic self and for believing in me even when I didn't believe in myself.

Jessie, our conversations all about baking were invaluable to me. These recipes would not have turned out the way they did without your knowledge and advice.

For my friends and recipe testers: I may have disguised this project as providing you with free, delicious food, but you all were doing me a huge favor. Thank you for trying, tasting, and giving me feedback along the way. Your satisfied smiles and words of encouragement kept me going and helped me believe in these recipes and in myself.

To my readers for inspiring me to write recipes and photograph food in the first place: My passion for sharing them always comes back to you.

To the Callisto Media team: Thank you for believing in me to bring this book's concept to life. Vanessa, I thought I knew how to write a recipe before, but your guidance through this process was helpful beyond words. Thank you.

About the Author

SARA McGLOTHLIN is a holistic nutrition and wellness coach, recipe creator, and food writer based in Richmond, Virginia. Ever since starting her first healthy-living blog in 2012, she has been passionate about inspiring and educating others on how to live healthier lives.

Sara also loves to cook, and her kitchen creations uphold her belief in the power of real, whole-food nutrition. She loves sharing recipes that are delicious, easy, and supportive of her readers' health—leaving them feeling nourished and satisfied. Additionally, her love of food photography has evolved into a passion for showing that healthy food can also be beautiful.

Before obtaining her certification as a holistic nutrition consultant, she worked in sales and marketing in both the banking and natural-foods industries. She graduated from the University of Virginia with a BA in economics and received her master's in elementary education from Mary Baldwin University. She is also a certified yoga teacher and barre instructor. You can visit her online at www.SaraMcGlothlin.com.